The Artist as a Channel

The Artist as a Channel

J. Donald Walters

Crystal Clarity, Publishers
14618 Tyler Foote Road
Nevada City, California 95959

Cover design by Bella Potapovskaya

Art, as I've used the word in this essay, refers to any esthetic medium that goes beyond the mechanical demands of mere craftsmanship and allows the artist to give outward expression to his inner feelings and states of consciousness.

Contents

Preface

When you look at a lake, what do you notice? the broad expanse of water, and the ripples on its surface? the surrounding trees and beaches? the people dotted about the surface, boating, fishing, and swimming?

When a biologist examines the lake's water under a microscope, what he sees is something very different: the teeming amoebae, paramecia, and other minute fauna that move about in their own little worlds.

And when a physicist thinks of the water, he may do so in still more microscopic terms — as molecules of whirling atoms, and as shining electrons dashing about with frenetic motion.

There are many ways to view any subject. The

broad view is often accused by those engrossed in a study of its minutiae as being too general, too vague and unspecific.

Any broad statement on art, similarly, is bound to become a target for such accusations. For it has little choice but to soar in a sweeping arc over the teeming mass of artistic "movements" and "isms," of theories and counter theories regarding fleeting issues of the moment, and to focus on far-ranging ideas that embrace all humanity. The concern of anyone making such a statement, indeed, must be more with mankind than even with the arts, as such. That is to say, he must approach the arts as expressions of human nature and human values, and not as subjects of study quite independent of the human beings who produce and enjoy them.

The microscopic view has its place, obviously. Many professional artists in every field, however, never ask themselves whether the arts bear any meaningful relationship to broad questions of human values. Writers can become so enamored of the well-turned phrase that they resent it if anyone asks them whether there is also some measure of truth in what they are saying. Violinists can become so engrossed in perfecting their bowing that they never ask themselves whether the music they are playing is more than technically worthwhile. And painters can become so bewitched by subtle gradations of color and by the inventiveness of their designs that they become outraged if you ask them whether their color schemes serve a broader purpose.

The amount of energy that people devote to lesser arguments in the arts is some indication of how little energy they may have to spare for greater themes.

Several years ago I made a comment to a friend about Schubert's melody for Shakespeare's song, "Hark, Hark! the Lark." It's a lovely melody. As I remarked to my friend, however, it does a disservice to Shakespeare's lyrics, at least in the original English. For although the first line of the lyrics scans properly as iambic, to read it you must give the first line a different emphasis, thus: *"Hark, hark! the lark at heaven's gate sings."* Only thus does one get a sense of a lark soaring upward at daybreak. Schubert, however, wrote the whole line as though it scanned conventionally: *"Hark, hark! the lark at heaven's gate sings."* Musically it's beautiful, but it betrays the lyrics.

"How fascinating," exclaimed my friend. "You know, I just read an article on that very point!" I hadn't known, but apparently someone thought enough of this point to make a bigger issue of it than I'd intended.

The difference in energy output between a casual statement and an entire article is considerable. And yet, whole careers have been dedicated to proving such theories.

Consider the famous Shakespeare vs. Sir Francis Bacon controversy. Again, consider the heat that has been generated by the champions of this artistic "ism" against that "ism": impressionism, postimpressionism, realism, surrealism, cubism, conceptualism, modernism — the list is endless.

People who are totally immersed in the minutiae of the world of art have developed a language as esoteric as that of any religious cult. It seems equally designed, moreover, to exclude the uninitiated. They will speak matter-of-factly of the "tension" between an artist's "conceptual approach to construction and the associational power of the objects he assembles." Perhaps they do not even want to be understood.

I think it is time we stepped back a little from the vast array of artistic "isms," and rethought what it is that the arts might express *for us all*, as human beings, rather than only privately — as they so often do — for the artist.

Such, then, is the purpose of this book: to give the overview; to concentrate on the lake in its broad relation to its surroundings, and not as an aggregate of teeming little drops. My purpose is to reach outward from the individual trends in the arts and feel through them the rhythms of life itself.

Chapter One

The Arts and Communication

In the center of a complex of little shops on the island of Kauai, a configuration of huge, painted pipes curves upward inside the bare framework of a tall tower, prevented from further upward growth by a high platform. The pipes look either like some complicated sewage system, or like the water supply system for a suburban community. Clearly, they are too large to serve only the small community of boutiques and souvenir shops that huddle around them, and over which they loom like some dragon awaiting his next maiden so he can get on with his dinner.

I endured the sight for two or three visits to the island. Finally I asked one of the shop owners, "When are they planning to cover those pipes?"

"Cover them? Why, what do you mean? That's sculpture!"

"You mean — they've actually been put there deliberately?"

"That's right," he replied proudly, as much as to say, "You see? We got everything here. Culture, too."

Okay — okay. But to me still those pipes are unlovely — to put it delicately. They are far too large among the little rows of one-storey shops that they dominate. They are completely inappropriate. And they are utterly meaningless.

The real issue at stake here, however, is not whether this particular product of an artist's loving fancy is really as ugly, inappropriate, and meaningless as it appears to me. The issue, rather, is whether I have any right to pass this judgment on them.

I may be within bounds in calling it ugly. Many people, however, would say that I had overstepped my limits even here. For in calling it ugly I imply that it ought to be something else. The artist, however, may have *wanted* to create something ugly. Maybe ugliness, for reasons unimaginable, was his particular statement. If so, is it my place to tell him he shouldn't make such a statement?

When I go on to suggest that heavy pipes, among all the quaint boutiques and shops selling picture post cards, are inappropriate, there are many who would tell me that I am pitting my purely personal judgment against that of the artist. Again, what right have I to do that?

But it is when I call the work meaningless that I really show myself capable of almost any crime.

"Why *should* a work of art have meaning?" Mentally I can hear the outraged demand. And:

"Why do you want it to make a statement? Why can't it just be itself?"

Well, I didn't say it had to make a statement. Lots of great art makes no statement at all. Look at the Mona Lisa. But even though it doesn't make any statement, it says something beautiful to me, and to enough other people besides for it to be counted among the greatest paintings in the world. No one has ever accused Leonardo of having created something meaningless, even though the admirers of his painting haven't yet managed, after five centuries, to decipher the meaning of that mysterious smile.

I call a work meaningless if it not only says nothing to me, but seems incapable of saying anything to anyone else. Sometimes I am mistaken in my judgment. We all have our blind spots. Tastes, moreover, vary. Even one's own tastes change from time to time. The point at issue here is: Where does the artist's personal statement end, and the public's right to understand it begin?

It should be self-evident that if a work of art is put on public display, it ought no longer to be accepted, perhaps with a shrug of the shoulders, as the artist's private secret. It should represent at least an effort on his part to communicate with others.

I don't mean that he has no right to protect his private life from the public. Obviously, deep, personal, and therefore private, experiences have been the inspiration for many, perhaps even for most, of the great works of art through the ages. Those aspects of an experience, however, which are too personal for public consumption ought to be translated into terms which others can understand and apply

15

to themselves.

In even the most intimate joys and griefs, there is always some aspect of them that can be shared meaningfully with others. One's grief in bereavement, for example, is a tragedy in which almost everyone can participate, provided that it isn't depicted in terms that are too particular to his own case.

People are always more interested in their own problems than in those of someone else, particularly someone they don't even know. An artist ought to reach out and touch them where their own interests lie. Any mature person would do as much. And for art to be accepted as truly great, it must display the sort of maturity that one associates with greatness.

There is a delicate balance to be achieved between intense personal feeling and the communication of that feeling to others in such a way as to enable them to share in it as well. Every artist must figure out for himself how best to accomplish this end. What I want to stress is only this: that there must be a conscious *effort* on the artist's part to communicate with his public. If there is no such effort, then the public's time ought not to be wasted in trying to figure out what it means.

If what I have said is true, and a work of art that is offered to the public ought to represent a sincere effort at communication on the artist's part, then we see crossed automatically off the map an incredible amount of work that has passed for art in this Twentieth Century. *For if there is one thing that marks whole schools of modern artistic thinking, it is the belief that communication doesn't matter.*

We might even go so far as to add that, if there is one thing that marks a great deal of modern art, it is a deliberate attempt on the part of the artists to confound their public.

I attended a piano concert a few months ago, while traveling. The concert was by someone who played, along with a selection of better-known pieces, several compositions of his own. It amazed me, listening to his own pieces, to see the lengths to which he had gone to impress us with his unpredictability — as though thereby alone to demonstrate his originality.

There was no sense of fitness in a single melodic line, nor in a single chord progression or rhythmic sequence. Just when one expected, and wanted, the melody to take one direction, it would leap off in some other — as much as to say, "Ha, ha! I fooled you, didn't I?" Just when a succession of dissonances cried out to resolve themselves finally in some friendly chord, the music would dash off north, south, east, or west — it didn't seem to matter where, as long as it left disaster in its wake. Rhythmic patterns that finally staggered off to a hesitant beginning would be hastily recalled and made to roam about uncertainly for a page or two in search of new directions.

Obviously, the whole thing was deliberate. Possibly the composer thought he was educating our musical tastes by shocking us out of our habit-born expectations. Apart from the intense dissatisfaction the pieces created in me, however, what I felt was that the composer was only trying to impress us with his cleverness, by offering musical choices that none of us could have expected. Subtly, he seemed to be telling us, "You can't fathom me. You see? I'm inscrutable! That makes me wiser than you."

Incomprehensibility is frequently offered not only to confound people, but to trick them into thinking that in the artist's vagueness, even confusion, they have finally encountered profundity — a profundity, one might add, in which the artist himself doesn't necessarily participate. In other words, incomprehensibility is generally an artist's way of concealing the fact that he has nothing to say.

No one before our modern era ever equated mere unpredictability with originality, and certainly never with genius. One of the profound satisfactions in listening to a Beethoven symphony is the sense of fitness it conveys. It isn't that Beethoven takes the opposite tack of being predictable; but, predictable or not, what he does is always right. It is what you would have wanted to do, had you possessed his genius.

This doesn't mean that for music to be great it needs to have a familiar ring. Sometimes, indeed, an artist — particularly one who is out of step with tradition — will make one work hard to tune in to what he is saying. If he is indeed saying something worthwhile, however, *and is clear himself about what he is saying,* people will come to learn his language in time, and to love it.

Normally, the test of greatness in the arts is the ability to state deep feelings and perceptions simply, clearly, and well.

Tolstoy, whose **War and Peace** has been acclaimed the greatest novel ever written, considered his simple folk tales artistically more valid exactly because of their extreme simplicity.

A certain famous writer made it a practice to read whatever he wrote to his father, who, though not a literary man, was richly endowed with common sense.

"I don't understand that passage," the father would complain.

"Well it simply means...." The son would go on to explain his meaning.

"Then why didn't you say so?" demanded the father.

The son would change the passage accordingly. He used to claim that his writing was always improved for his father's insistence that he make it simpler and clearer.

Indeed, it might well be said that until a person can express a thought simply and clearly, he hasn't yet understood it clearly himself.

Instead, however — and unfortunately — obscurity has become the vogue. The artist feels superior to others, because most people admit frankly that they can't understand him. And he feels sustained also, because enough people are willing to demonstrate their own superiority to the artistically unsophisticated by claiming that they do understand him. It is like the story of the Emperor's suit of clothes.

How did things get to be the way they are?

Chapter Two

The Artist as Visionary

1859 was the year of a monumental event in the history of science: the publication of Charles Darwin's *Origin of Species*. Countless assumptions of modern thought have developed out of Darwin's carefully worked-out theory of evolution, which he traced through many examples to a process of natural selection.

In 1858, one year earlier, there occurred another monumental event, one that may eventually prove more important than the appearance of Darwin's work. To Bernadette Soubirous, the oldest child of one of the poorest families of Lourdes, France, there appeared in a vision a beautiful lady. The lady, after a number of successive appearances, told Bernadette, "I am The Immaculate Conception."

Instructed by the lady, Bernadette dug with her hands in the ground at a spot near where the visions were taking place, and a miraculous spring welled up. Since then, in the waters of this spring, many medically authenticated miracles of healing have occurred.

There are two reasons why these appearances may prove to have been of even greater importance than the publication of Darwin's theory.

First, a few disconcerting cracks have begun to appear in the solid wall of scientific support for Darwinism. So far, the wall seems still to be holding firm. After more than a century, however, and in defiance of the most fundamental claim of Darwinian evolution, no genuine fossil evidence has yet been found to link one species to another. This discouraging fact has been causing ripples of serious doubt in scientific circles.

Given the further fact that science is prone to throw overboard every few years some of its basic, most universally accepted theories, one cannot but wonder whether Darwin's theory, too, may not end up on the rubbish heap.

In this case, certainly, the appearances of the Virgin Mary at Lourdes will become more important, not only for the lasting healing powers of the spring, but for a more far-reaching reason. For if Darwin should be discredited, the whole scientific dogma of accidental evolution will have to be reevaluated from the bottom up. Deliberate divine intervention in earthly affairs may even gain serious plausibility among thinking people — a possibility which, so far, they would dismiss as ludicrous.

The second reason for the importance of the Madonna's appearances has to do with their long-range effect on the overall consciousness of mankind.

The appearances at Lourdes were quite possibly the first of their kind in the history of Christianity: a vision intended for the general upliftment, not of a few devotees and mystics, but of all humanity, complete with demonstrations, medically verified, of divine power. These manifestations occurred not during the Middle Ages, when people generally believed in at least the possibility of miracles. The appearances coincided, rather, with the very height of the age of scientific materialism. In this context, don't they take on the aspect of a divine answer — both to science and to science-inspired materialism?

The miracles themselves deal with a perfectly material reality: physical illness. They demonstrate a power that medical science cannot duplicate. The results are scientifically verifiable. The Madonna's appearances, in other words, meet both science and modern materialism on their own ground — not with a call to forsake the world and enter a life of renunciation and prayer, but with a call to humanity in general to depend more on God, and less on self-vaunted but fragile human capabilities.

For the visions, and their practical consequences, testified to a higher reality than that of matter. Implicitly, they were a call to embrace spiritual values — and at a time when the West as a whole was beginning to doubt whether any such values existed.

The pertinent point in the story of St. Bernadette,

where this book is concerned, is that something already existed in the mass consciousness during the Nineteenth Century that repudiated the claims of materialism. Had this not been the case, it is doubtful that the visions at Lourdes would have taken place, for God's way has never been to impose Himself on mankind.

The Romantic Movement in the arts, too, was a reaction against the arid implications of scientific materialism. It was a reaction also against the ugliness of the more dehumanizing aspects of the Industrial Revolution.

The poet, John Keats, wrote, "There was a rainbow once in heaven. Now it is listed in the catalogue of common things." Sensitive spirits *wanted* some sort of inner vision that would substantiate their intuitive feeling that higher realities existed. They shrank from the fact-centered findings of science, which seemed slowly to be squeezing all sense of wonder out of existence.

Very few of these artists were spiritually inclined. At any rate, few were deeply so. The need for some sort of vision was there, and they felt it. But their response to the need was human, not divine. Far from praying for divine intervention, their proposal for an antidote to materialism lay in the arts. Gradually, for them, the arts became their religion.

In place of divine visions — invisible except to the visionary — they proposed visions about life and reality that, in their exaggerated sensitivity, set them outside the teeming marketplace of ordinary, crass businessmen and scientists, and made of them the priests and priestesses in a new cult. If people failed to appreciate their artistic sensibilities — well, wasn't it too much to expect that any but true artistic visionaries, like themselves, would be able to share in their inspiration?

The Romantic Movement created the myth of the artist as a rare being, a creature of exquisite spiritual refinement, gifted with special insights into the nature of reality. Naturally, it was in the interests of these rare beings to perpetuate the myth.

Lest anyone think I am jeering, I should explain that it is as an artist that I am writing this book.

Even today, many people consider artists to be blessed with insights that are denied the common ruck of humanity.

A certain lady of my acquaintance, a successful musician, once posed me this rhetorical question: "What could be more spiritual than music?" She was confident that I would agree with her, as a composer myself. Not wanting to argue, I left the subject with a mumbled, "Mmmm."

But is music, in itself, really spiritual? Would anyone place martial music in the same camp as Handel's *Messiah*? Some music is inspiring; other music is depressing, even decadent.

The arts can express values. They are not, however, values in themselves. And this is one of the points of confusion that have arisen since artists began publicly to assume the role of visionaries.

This pseudo-mystical role is only one of three main tributaries that feed into the current of opinion which sets artistic self-expression in opposition to artistic communication.

Chapter Three

The Arts and the Subconscious

In 1856, three years before the publication of Darwin's theory of evolution, a man was born who was destined to have a major impact on people's understanding of the way the subconscious mind operates. Others, including Immanuel Kant, had already written about the subconscious. It was Sigmund Freud, however, who made the first scientific study of this little-understood aspect of human consciousness.

Since near the end of the Nineteenth Century, when Freud began publishing his psychological findings, the subconscious may be said virtually to have come into its own in human thought.

No more natural field existed for the expression of Freud's theories, and of the related theories of others, than the arts. It may be said that the salient difference between the artistic and the scientific method has always been that, whereas science tries to exclude all influence from the subconscious mind, in the arts the influence of the subconscious is actively courted.

The very purpose of the arts is to touch us, not only at the conscious level, but at our deepest subconscious levels of being. Were it not for our need to be emotionally involved as well as intellectually, we might have preferred it had Francois Villon simply said, "Time passes." Why, we might have asked, did he repeat at the end of every stanza of his "Ballad of Ladies of Olden Times" the refrain: "But where are the snows of yesteryear?" (*"Mais ou sont les neiges d'antan?"*)

Shakespeare wrote, in **A Midsummer Night's Dream**:

"The poet's eye, in a fine frenzy rolling,
Doth glance from heaven to earth, from earth to
    heaven;
And as imagination bodies forth
The forms of things unknown, the poet's pen
Turns them to shapes and gives to airy nothing
A local habitation and a name."

Had he been writing a sociological study, he might have said merely, "Poets have a lot of imagination."

Mozart, instead of telling us to be joyful, wrote music that touches our imaginations and makes us *feel* joyful. Botticelli, instead of depicting spring literally, with crocuses on the ground and fresh leaves appearing on the trees, painted young maidens dancing in a mood of springtime, and a fanciful zephyr, humanized, blowing the air above them. He touched our *feelings* about springtime; that is why his **Primavera** is so deservedly famous.

The ancient Greeks, too, though amazingly realistic in their sculptures, yet offered poses of dignity and grace that one rarely beholds in life. Their work was idealized; it sprang from deeper currents of human consciousness than it could have, had the artists merely been depicting human beings as they were.

Between the contributions of Darwin and Freud, however, a new concept has forced its way into human thinking. People no longer view the subconscious merely as a vast subcontinent that constitutes far more of our total awareness than we consciously realize. Rather, the subnormal (in the case of Darwin) and the abnormal (in the case of Freud) have been foisted upon us as our basic human realities. This is the sort of exaggeration that always seems to go hand in hand with new discoveries.

If we really are only primates "out on a limb," so to speak, then of course it follows that any effort to refine human nature must make us seem as ludicrous as a clown would be, trying to pose as a king.

And if we really are our lower nature, and nothing but our lower nature, then altruistic love can only be what Freud said it was: a manifestation of suppressed lust. As well expect a beetle to croon love songs as expect a person really to mean it when he speaks of being inspired.

The normal Freudian advice, in fact, for anyone caught in a conflict between his higher and lower natures is to side at once with the lower. For it is only in our lower selves that we have any hope of ever achieving complete self-integration.

The subconscious mind is irrational. It hasn't the slightest interest in communication. And it's "where the action is" — if indeed the subconscious is the reality for which the conscious is merely a coverup.

Here, then, we see the second of the tributaries that have been feeding into the mainstream of modern art. Armed with the belief that only the outpourings of the subconscious mind can express who we really are, the artist has carte blanche to take his work in any direction at all, and claim that he is engaged in a search for "truth." If we complain we can't seem to relate to his work, he feels justified in replying that that is simply because we haven't been granted his particular vision.

In certain primitive societies, madmen were considered divinely inspired. There has always been a certain confusion in people's minds about the difference between madness and inspiration, particularly where real inspiration was not encountered.

I don't know whether the thought has already been verbalized by someone else, but certainly it would seem that people who are mad or abnormal must be in a strong position nowadays to gain recognition as great artists. To mad people, subconscious expression comes naturally; it isn't something they have to work at perfecting. The arts, moreover, offer them the ideal field in which to express their "talents." Once all objective criteria, and common sense as well, have been removed from the jury bench, all that such artists need in order to get themselves accepted is a certain sweep and vigor. And an uncontrolled sweep and vigor are often the salient characteristics of mental disease.

We owe it to ourselves not to be fooled by rationalizations, no matter how clever they are. The rationalizations can have Freud's name attached to them, or any other famous person's for that matter. Whatever the credentials, if their claim defies common sense, then it should at least be examined with a certain caution. The ancient Romans had a saying for it: *Caveat emptor* — "Let the buyer beware."

That Freud made certain important discoveries is undeniable. Suppression obviously does play an important part in human psychology. The subconscious mind may even play a more important role in human life than the psychologists themselves realize.

Yet it is the conscious mind that filters what comes up from the subconscious. It is the conscious mind that refines and directs the impulses it receives. And it is the conscious mind, finally, that can gradually change harmful subconscious impulses.

To believe otherwise would be to give free rein to every impulse — homicidal, vengeful, suicidal; it wouldn't matter. A lot of psychology, indeed, claims that to give free rein to such impulses in some non-harmful situation, such as painting it out on canvas, serves as a kind of therapy. What such expression also does, however, is give emphasis to the attitudes it is expressing. It affirms them. The relief is temporary. In the long term, the habit only becomes more deeply imbedded in the mind.

It would be the sheerest madness to ask insane people to set the tone for society. Why, then, do so many leading figures in the arts propound theories that escape being equated with insanity only because they are expounded rationally? The exposition of them is rational, but the artistic expression of them is not. And in this century, particularly, a betrayal of society everywhere on the part of its intellectuals has been their deliberate use of reason to confound common sense.

The basic problem stems from the belief that evolution has driven us forward — that, in the mere struggle to survive, mankind has developed hands, a brain, and what he is pleased to call his finer sensibilities. He is believed to have been pushed upward from below. Therefore, he would have developed no interest in beauty, love, happiness, or wisdom had it not been for his instinctual need to eat, to procreate, and to protect himself from being eaten in turn.

The basic dogma of our time is that we are all predators at heart, grunting cavemen at heart, rapists and destroyers at heart. The purest expression of true humanity is believed to be the basic laborer, or, alternatively, the person who lives unthinkingly, by his instincts alone.

Here is an ironic question: Could it really be only a basic *insincerity* regarding who they really are that has led great men and women to devote their entire lives to a search for truth?

The whole modern approach to human realities has begun to seem sterile. When a belief system fails to work, the only sensible thing to do is abandon it and look for some other system. And the present belief system is not working at all, if by "working" we mean, Is it leading us anywhere, and has it proved constructive? The only direction it has led us so far is down an ever-narrowing lane that seems to be heading toward a dead end.

When one alternative fails, one automatically looks to its opposite for a solution. Perhaps this is what we ought to do in the present predicament. What about looking upon human progress, not as a push upward from below, but as a magnetic attraction from above? What if love, and not lust, be the reality? In this case, instead of love being a mere cloak for animal lust, lust, rather, would be an inchoate reaching out for its perfection in love.

One of the things taught in physics is that potential energy is every bit as real as kinetic energy. By the same token, may we not say that if pure love, or radiant joy, or divine aspiration is a part of some people's present reality, then these qualities were in existence — potentially, and therefore in reality — from the time, billions of years ago, when the first atoms united to produce stars?

May we not say, too, that evolution is due at least as much to a reaching out in aspiration as it is to the desperate urge to survive?

This explanation has, if nothing else, at least this much going for it: that it leads out onto ever expanding vistas, and not into the ever-narrowing lane, leading toward a dead end, in which we presently find ourselves.

Where the arts are concerned, exaggerated emphasis on the subconscious has produced neither clarity nor self-understanding. These, at least, must have been the fruits looked for out of so much dedication to unveiling man's true nature. Surely it is time that we gave the conscious mind its due once again — and not the conscious mind only, but the aspirations of that mind toward the heights of potential experience, both human and divine.

Chapter Four

The Arts and Relativity

The most fertile years in the life of Sigmund Freud were from 1895 to 1900. It was during those years that he did some of his most important research on the subconscious, a vast labor which culminated in the publication, in 1900, of his major work, *The Interpretation of Dreams.*

By an interesting coincidence, it was those same years, from 1895 to 1900, that marked a major turning point in physical science. As J. W. N. Sullivan wrote in his great book, *The Limitations of Science,* "The modern era may be said to have begun about the year 1895. Between that year and the year 1900 those researches were begun which have changed our whole conception of matter and which have, further, changed our whole idea of the meaning and purpose of physical science. So great a revolution in scientific thought has not occurred since Copernicus showed that the earth went round the sun."

This revolution began with the discovery of the electron. Gradually it became clear to physicists that the fundamental nature of the universe is not material, that the matter we think of as solid is basically insubstantial: energy, in fact, and not really matter at all.

Soon, Albert Einstein was declaring that time is relative. The "necessary truths" of logic — the clear axioms, for instance, of Euclidean geometry — were admitted not to be necessities at all. Before very long, scientists were beginning to doubt whether there are any "necessary truths" in existence. They stopped looking for truth through their sciences, and began seeking merely workable solutions.

The impact of science on non-scientific thought was profound. No one seemed to know what to make of a universe in which none of the familiar rules any longer applied. Absolute principles began giving way, in the minds of many thinking people, to a philosophy of relativity which they applied to human values as much as to the Einsteinian universe. If no "necessary truths" could be found in logic or in physical science, this could only mean, according to them, that truth itself doesn't exist. If no clear purpose could be discerned in the universe, this meant that everything is purposeless. And if logic and reason are merely human inventions, everything must therefore be illogical — or, in other words, meaningless.

Meaninglessness thus became a cornerstone of

modern philosophical thought. The rejection of absolute values began with the claim that values are relative. In time, it developed into a more cynical insistence that human values, like truth itself, don't even exist. People began justifying every conceivable type of antisocial behavior with the rationale, "Nothing means anything anyway, so why shouldn't a person do just as he wants? All that matters is that he be able to get away with it."

The Twentieth Century has had to deal with the problem of how to relate to a universe in which so many seemingly fundamental realities have been disproved.

Well, we'll probably resolve it all in time, emerging smilingly into sunlight at the other end of the tunnel. After all, there is no reason whatever to assume that, if things don't mean exactly what we thought they meant, they can't therefore mean anything else, either.

What we are going through, obviously, is a process of philosophical readjustment. If historical precedent is any guideline, one consequence of this readjustment will probably be an expanded vision of reality: a broader — non-dogmatic, for example — definition of values, and deeper faith in man's place in the universal scheme of things. There is no good reason to believe, on the basis of what we know so far about the nature of reality, that it will turn out that there is nothing left for us to believe in any more. It would be frivolous, surely, on the basis of the evidence submitted to date, to insist that the entire basis of our faith has been destroyed.

Meanwhile — what of the arts? Artistic expression requires an imaginative evaluation of the facts it takes into consideration. An artist is obliged by the very nature of his calling to be more than gently puzzled by so great a philosophical challenge as meaninglessness. He must build on the information, like a child lying in bed at night who creates witches and dragons out of the shadows cast by a street light onto the wall of his bedroom.

In this respect, indeed, one might say that the arts have outdone themselves in the way they've responded to the challenge. They have turned meaninglessness into the final cry of despair wrung from the hearts of a betrayed humanity; into some noisome swamp of cosmic indifference, the miasma of which is stretching out its tentacles to poison all of life. Artistic reactions have ranged from shaking pens, flutes, and brushes in helpless rage at the injustice of it all, and from impatient cries for total destruction (followed, some dare hope, by a new beginning), to manic glee over the absurdity of everything; from poetic lamentations over the eternal loneliness of man to the jeering conclusion that the arts have no other mission than to tweak him for wanting things any different.

As a general statement, one may say on looking back that all the reactions seem to have been negative. They have built on a situation that is admittedly bleak, but one that requires calm consideration if a solution is to be found. Like village gossips when the parson's daughter ran away with the local playboy, they have created such a tempest of emotional anguish that it is difficult even to speak for all the branches hurtling through the air about one's head.

Inevitably, creative people in every department of the arts have gone in one of two directions: either toward blasphemy, or toward trivia. Some of them have embraced both of these at once.

Naturally, if life really is meaningless then there isn't much left for the artist to communicate, except maybe his own sense of helplessness and frustration, or the outraged declaration that everything really is without any meaning. Meaninglessness alone, however, isn't much of a message, especially when everyone else is working at his own embellishments of the same theme. Artists, moreover, generally feel their work ought to express at least *some* sort of meaning, if only to lift it a notch above the level of leatherwork, Easter-egg painting, and other branches of the lowly handicrafts.

Combining a sense of meaninglessness with their already established purpose of giving free rein to their subconscious, and with their long-held view of the artist as visionary, has produced a confusion of intentions that has left the artists themselves not completely sure whether they've really said anything or not, or whether they even wanted to. They want you to think they've said something. On the other hand, they don't want you to think anything of the kind. They want you to *feel* their work. In fact, they hope by studied vagueness to appear profound, and by intuitive forays into strange shapes, colors, or sounds to touch you deeply, whether or not they themselves have been similarly moved by their creations.

A few years ago at an art exhibit I saw an unprepossessing piece of welded metal titled "Fourth Allegory." An allegory, of course, has a specific meaning — implied, though not overtly stated. Unable to fathom the meaning of this work, I asked the sculptor, who was sitting beside it, what it meant.

"It has no meaning," he replied. Seeing me about to press him for an explanation, he continued, "It's similar, if you like, to the Zen Buddhistic idea: 'It is what it is.'"

Well, the peace-inspiring Zen Buddhistic meditation gardens I'd seen in Japan were certainly allegorical statements. They depicted wide expanses of sea; long, rolling waves; and rocky islands scattered artistically about on the surface. Obviously, if this sculptor's work wasn't an allegory for anything, it ought to have been named something else.

Why, then, did he choose this name — and call it the *fourth* allegory at that? Evidently, because he wanted the best of both worlds. He wanted to seem to be making a statement, while not confining himself to any statement at all. He wanted to imply meaning on one level, while at the same time saying, "No, it isn't at that level that you can find its meaning." This kind of uncertainty on the artist's part as to his own intentions is generally excused on all the three grounds that I've outlined in these last three chapters.

The arts, however, serve a true function — at least where the public is concerned — only when they can clarify for people their own hopes and dreams, their doubts and longings, their deepest feelings about life and death and the hereafter. The arts serve an even greater function if they can suggest clarity in matters where most people see confusion.

They can serve none of these functions, however, if the artists themselves are confused.

If the arts are ever to get back into the business of expressing the things people generally would like to express, if only they knew how, they must be directed toward the rediscovery of mental clarity. And if artists are ever again to express feelings and insights that will touch people profoundly, I think they themselves need to spend less time at their easels, pianos, or typewriters, and more time learning how to live with themselves. They need to devote time to learning how to achieve greater clarity in their lives, and deeper — because clearer — feeling. Perhaps, above all, they need to develop spiritual insight.

Too many artists nowadays are like boats adrift on an uncharted sea. They are like people running so urgently in search of something that they haven't the time to stop and see whether they don't have it already, in their own pocket.

Isn't it time, now, for a return to clarity?

Chapter Five

What Is Clarity?

This story is told of George Fredrick Handel, when he was composing the *Messiah*: His meals, which were left outside the room where he worked, went for some days untouched. After several days, the person who brought them daily, concerned for Handel's welfare, opened the door and looked in. And there he found the composer weeping for sheer joy, so inspired was he by the beauty of the music that was coming through him.

After completing his famous "Hallelujah" chorus, Handel is said to have exclaimed ecstatically, "I did think I did see all Heaven before me, and the great God Himself!"

Like most music lovers in the Western world, I myself have attended many performances of the

Messiah over the years, and have listened to it many more times on recordings. As for many others, I imagine, there have been times when I, too, was moved to tears by my joy in the music. On certain occasions the beauty of this oratorio has caused my body to be covered in goose bumps at the sheer thrill I felt.

Here, however, is an important point to ponder: Could my joy ever equal Handel's, who stood at the very fountain of that inspiration while composing the *Messiah?* I very much doubt it. If indeed my inspiration had ever equaled his, its source would have had to lie within myself, and not in his music.

For all artistic creation is like water flowing downhill: Whatever point it reaches after its first emergence onto the mountainside can only be downhill from its initial source. Artistic expression might in fact be defined as *filtered inspiration.*

Observe the genesis of a work of art.

First, there is the filter of the artist's mind. For whatever his feeling or inspiration, he must himself tune in to it and understand it to the best of his ability. The highest potentials of an inspiration are not defined or limited by the person who receives it.

Second comes the medium the artist uses, in which he must somehow capture as well as possible the intensity of his own feelings and inspiration. Therein, of course, lies his skill as an artist. Perfection, at this stage of expression, is impossible. For no one can commit exactly to mere canvas or paper anything so insubstantial as the will-o'-the-wisp of inspiration.

Third, at least in the case of music and writing,

comes the consciousness of the people who present the work: the soloists, the conductor, the musicians; or, in the case of an author, his editor and publisher, even his printer. Sculptors and painters may not seem to have this third filter to deal with, but in fact the atmosphere of the room where their works are displayed also influences the impact of their work on the viewer. Composers and playwrights, however, are in the worst situation at this stage, for they are almost wholly at the mercy of their interpreters, some of whom may contrive to turn the most joyous piece of music into something resembling a dirge. Authors, too, can have the impact of their work seriously diluted even by something as trivial-seeming as the wrong choice of type fonts.

Fourth in the process comes the filter of criticism, whether favorable or unfavorable. For at this point the work often becomes shrouded by an almost impenetrable veil of opinion, through which other people can hardly experience the work any more as a thing in itself.

Fifth, and lastly, there is the artist's public. A work of art may lay bare his soul, but if the person viewing it has just eaten hot dogs with mustard and relish and is feeling a bit queasy; or if he has a child tugging at his arm, pleading, "Let's go eat, Daddy!"; or if, glancing at the work, he thinks, "Impressionists — bah!" without giving this particular impressionist an opportunity to explain himself: What chance has the poor artist for a fair appraisal?

Considering all these unavoidable filters for the artist's initial inspiration, think how great that inspiration needs to be in order to preserve even a glimmer of its original light by the time it reaches its destination at the public's eye, or ear. Perhaps this, too, is why many artists try to offer form, sound, and color as substitutes for an inspiration they themselves don't even try to feel, and claim that their work itself *is* the inspiration they're offering.

Is it possible for forms, colors, sounds, and words alone to inspire one, or to affect one deeply, even if no deep experience went into producing them?

The great Indian mystic, Sri Ramakrishna, had his first experience of *samadhi*, or ecstasy, as a young man while watching a flock of geese flying against a grey cloud. The beauty of the scene moved him so profoundly that for a time he lost all sense of outer reality, while his mind plunged into a heaven of inner joy.

Did those geese have any consciousness of the effect they were producing in that one young man on the ground below? One assumes that they were totally unaware of his reaction.

Again, a friend of mine, herself a musician, once attended a concert given in a national park by a young violinist of distinctly unprofessional skill. My friend had entered the park that day fairly singing with inner bliss — that special feeling of upliftment which people occasionally feel, though all too rarely, in their lives.

"Wasn't the music heavenly!" she exclaimed to her companions after the concert.

"Heavenly?" they replied in astonishment. "Why, that boy didn't even play in tune!"

How had it happened that this woman, perfectly capable of distinguishing a good performance from a bad one, was so deeply moved by such an obviously mediocre performance? The answer is clear: She had projected her own inner feelings onto the music, as she found herself doing onto all her surroundings that day.

The answer, then, to the question of whether one can be inspired by a work of art even if the artist himself shares none of the inspiration, is, "Yes, one can, but in this case the artist deserves no share of the credit. For the source of the person's inspiration lies in himself. He might have been moved quite as deeply by gazing at a pebble, or a tree."

There is no getting around it: If an artist wants to reach people on any level whatsoever, he must first reach up (or down, as the case may be) to that level himself. He can't expect to carry a torch through the rains of every filtering influence, if the "torch" itself is only a sputtering match.

The artist must, in other words, be very clear about what he himself is trying to express, whether it be verbally, visually, or aurally. Vague impressions will simply translate themselves, whether on canvas or in the concert hall, as even vaguer impressions.

Many an artist has given voice to his feelings in words something like these: "Well, man, I was standing up there on that mountaintop — you know what I mean? — and suddenly it hit me, like, you know, things just don't have to be the way they are." No? Please tell me, how are things, anyway? And why don't they have to be the way they are? Moreover, how else might they be?

An artist doesn't have to have rational answers

to these questions. After all, he isn't supposed to write a philosophical essay on whatever moves him. He might even make some such statement as the one above, incoherent as it seems when verbalized, with a perfectly clear conception of what he is really trying to say. It may simply be that, for him, his clarity comes when he's standing before a canvas, or thinking in terms of melodies and chord progressions. All this is quite possible, though certainly by his words alone he gives no hint that such is the case. Clarity on *some* level of his awareness, however, is essential.

I remember a time several years ago, when I was composing an oratorio titled, **Christ Lives**. During that time, I was so immersed in music as my focus of expression that I found it difficult even to tune in to the patterns of human speech. One evening I had to host a previously scheduled dinner party. People addressed me at the table, and I would stare at them almost as if in bewilderment before knowing what to say in reply. One of my guests, a friend of many years' standing, remarked to me later that she'd had the feeling I was asking myself, while trying to think of an answer, "Now, is she a B flat?"

Music is its own language, one that isn't easily translated into human speech. Perhaps I'd have answered my friend better had I burst into song!

That is why the play and movie, **Amadeus**, was so embarrassingly inadequate in its portrayal of Mozart. For even if young Amadeus did use foul or childish language (and I'm not inclined to put much faith in this statement that he did), words were not the medium of self-expression that he'd cultivated.

Speech, to some extent, for him was like an alien tongue, with all the frustration that trying to speak it might induce.

Painting and sculpture are still other languages. Who can explain why a certain sweeping line may convey a sense of happiness, or another, a sense of loneliness, sorrow, or despair? It happens. No one can deny that it happens, if ever he has entered deeply into attunement with human expression through the visual arts. But who can explain, except after the fact, *how* it happens? Any artist so uninspired as to think, "Eureka! I have the formula!" would find that no amount of effort to reproduce that identical linear sweep could ever produce an identical effect.

Look at the movies put out by Disney Studios since the death of the artist. Walt Disney was, in his way, a genius. He labored with infinite patience and sensitivity over many years to produce what were truly works of art in their own right. He had to discover for himself the rules of this art. What he passed on to his successors was an impressive legacy of creative fantasy, and of techniques for evoking that sense of fantasy in children — and, for that matter, in adults. It is easy to see, in the films that have come out from Disney Studios since that time, their skillful use of his techniques. Yet somehow his inspiration is lacking.

There may even be a factor here that one can't explain — except perhaps in terms of vibrations. I'll never forget seeing the Mona Lisa for the first time at the Louvre, in Paris. I had seen it often already, expertly reproduced, in books and photographs. I'd always known the painting was beautiful. When I saw it in the original, however, I was moved beyond description. Nothing could have prepared me for the impact I felt, standing before that actual painting.

It's as if the arts had some kind of life of their own. I remember seeing also the Taj Mahal for the first time. Its sheer size, of course, may account for much of the wonder one feels on viewing it. But surely there's more to it. How breathtaking the sight is, as one stands before it in Agra! No model, no photograph could begin to convey the sensation.

Go to Delphi, in Greece, if ever you get the chance. Stand in what, by now, are only ruins. *Feel* the place: Don't merely stare at it. I can't imagine that you won't be moved by the experience.

People who ride the crest of a fad may paint blue paintings just "because blues are *in* now." They may compose dissonant symphonies because dissonances are "avant-garde." But going at it that way, they'll never be able to produce anything worthwhile.

Whatever one wants to express, regardless of his medium of expression, can be stated successfully only if he is very clear in himself as to what he wants to say.

An interesting phenomenon of verbal communication is the fact that one of the best methods for getting a clear answer is to state the question clearly. A well-stated problem is already halfway to its solution. In whatever artistic creativity one engages, he will find, similarly, that the greatest block to creativity occurs not when he is tired, nor even when the inspiration doesn't seem to want to come. It occurs when he isn't clear in himself as to what he wants to express.

Once the clarity is there, the inspiration flows.

Clarity means asking the right questions. It means knowing exactly what the problem is, and then offering that problem up into the creative flow, in the full expectation of receiving a solution.

Clarity is one-pointed concentration. Nothing great can be produced in the arts without complete attention, any more than a camera can take a clear picture if the lens is out of focus.

Clarity is also a condition for concentration. For no camera can take a clear picture if the lens is covered with dust.

Clarity is the first step to true inspiration. It is, indeed, the channel through which all true inspiration comes.

If, then, an artist wants to improve his work, he will do well to devote himself, not only to the work itself, but to developing his own powers of concentration, his own inner clarity.

And thus we come to one of the basic concepts of this book: *No inspiration is possible in the arts except that which descends from the artist's own, inner inspiration.*

Chapter Six

Clarity Means Expanding Awareness

A lady once was listening to someone reading the lusty "Miller's Tale," from Chaucer's *Canterbury Tales*, in the original Middle English.

"Why, it's beautiful!" she cried. "If only I understood it."

The reader pulled out another volume from the bookcase beside him, and began reading to her a translation of the same story into Modern English. Halfway through the reading, she cried out, "Stop! Please stop right there. Oh, if only I hadn't understood it!"

Clarity is important in any undertaking. Sometimes, however, it can be embarrassing. Many a modern painting that is now displayed proudly in the living room would be rushed up to the attic, were it understood!

More often, however, any attempt to clarify the meaning of a work of art would simply reveal that it had no meaning.

I can remember times when I've thought that what I was producing, whether musically or in words, was going beautifully. But then, as I worked to make it simpler and clearer, I discovered to my dismay that, stripped down to its essence, it stood revealed as nonsense.

It is no easier to face lack of clarity in one's work than it is in oneself. The one is a reflection of the other. It is important, however, to try one's best.

I met a lady once — her name was Nancy Ponch, God rest her soul; I used to call her my best critic — who had the job of introducing me at a concert I was once invited to give of my own songs. Nancy liked the songs well enough, and had the training besides, to offer me some insightful suggestions afterwards regarding the lyrics.

I was delighted with her advice, so much so that from then on, whenever I wrote another song, I would phone her and read her the words. It was agony when she insisted — as she often did — that a line I'd worked on so hard wasn't clear. I would expostulate, "But Nancy, listen to any song at all. Listen to many classical songs. They all have at least a line or two that sacrifices clarity to tonal beauty."

"Those are their weak points," she would reply, remorselessly. "They ought to have both clarity *and* beauty. They have enough else going for them, which is why they make it in spite of their flaws. But why not correct a flaw if it's obviously there?" And so, back I went to my desk. And back I came to her the next time I'd written a song. For no one else was willing, or competent, to help me learn how to achieve what I myself wanted to achieve: a combination of clarity *and* beauty.

One thing becomes increasingly obvious as one works to develop clarity in one's thinking. (And it is, of course, in the mind that clarity in the arts begins.) This is that mental confusion and negative states of mind have a great deal in common.

A person will cling to the thought, for example, "Life is no damn good," only as long as he doesn't sincerely ask himself, "Why not?"

Socrates believed that everyone, if he could be led by calm, impersonal discussion to the clear truth of a matter, would voluntarily forsake evil. For, as he said, true happiness lies only in virtue.

One reason that so many works of art in this century are expressions of negative attitudes is, quite simply, that they lack clarity. For not only does confusion disguise negativity: It is itself a negative state — even as outward disorder in a home is often a sign that the owner hasn't the courage to face up to the problems in his life. Confusion denotes low energy. So also does negativity.

It should be apparent by now that in emphasizing clarity I do not necessarily mean the clarity of Socratic logic. Socrates offered logic as his example of clarity, but another kind of clarity can be achieved just as surely through the feelings. A clear intuition, indeed, is always far more perceptive than a clear thought.

Clear feelings are expansive. They reach out to embrace other people's realities, to include them in one's own. Confused, muddy, and negative feelings are contractive. They exclude other people from their sympathies, and recognize others' feelings only in a spirit of denial.

The arts offer, above all, an opportunity to achieve clarity on a feeling level. The more one seeks sincerely to clarify — and not merely to affirm — one's feelings, the more positive, necessarily, they become.

It is easy to express strong negative feelings, and to convince oneself in the process that these feelings are deep. This is something like increasing the force of the jet of water through a hose by squeezing the hose at the tip. Negative emotions constrict the flow of feeling. They limit themselves to specific objects, and focus narrowly on the particular moment. Thus, the rage or indignation expressed seems strong because of its very violence. Violence, however, only destroys; it doesn't create. Violent feelings, moreover, are generally a sign of fundamental weakness, not of real strength at all.

The other way of increasing the flow of water in a hose is to open the faucet wider. Similarly, the alternative — and certainly the more constructive — way to strengthen the flow of feeling is to open wide one's heart to others.

If one will work to achieve clarity in his own life, and outwardly in his artistic expression, he will find himself naturally becoming a channel for positive states of mind.

Three chapters ago we discussed the dangers of

giving free rein to the subconscious mind. Many people, while granting the disadvantages of self-expression that is incoherent, would insist that opening oneself to the flow of inspiration from the subconscious has also produced some of the greatest inspirations of genius.

Let us see to what extent this is really so.

Is it not true that in subconsciousness we become passive — that, in a very real sense, we shut out from our minds the struggles of life, and withdraw from objective reality? Great inspirations come during periods of inner rest, of relaxation and withdrawal; there is no record, however, that they are consistent with a sense of passivity. Certainly, if they have come during passivity, they have also generated instantly in the mind an intense, dynamic, and completely positive state of consciousness. Great geniuses have always been men and women of much greater than normal awareness. Never have they been people who wandered about with a vacant gaze, as though drugged.

Great composers and other inspired geniuses have often remarked, as Handel did after writing the "Hallelujah" chorus, that it was as if their inspirations, when they had them, came to them from some higher source. The inspirations didn't seem even to originate in their own minds.

Brahms stated that if an inspiration was merely mind-born, it was of a lower order.

Is it possible that there is a higher aspect of human consciousness, as yet not investigated by science — a superconscious, as opposed to the subconscious mind which Freud investigated? It is, at any rate, definitely true that the inspirations that people have believed came to them through their openness to the subconscious came in fact not when they were in that frame of mind which invites subconscious influences, but when their minds were, in a sense, opened *upward*, or *outward*; when they were very clear in their minds as to what they wanted, and very positive in their effort to attune themselves to what they wanted.

Whatever one may call this aspect of the mind's function, its existence is a fact, well demonstrated in the life of every man and woman of genius, and in every person of extraordinary ability.

Again, the key word here is *clarity* — *Crystal Clarity*, if you will. For *Crystal Clarity* suggests that kind of clarity which enhances, instead of merely transmitting passively. It suggests clarity combined with beauty, with heightened awareness and inspiration.

Chapter Seven

Clarity Means Tuning In

I once went with a group of friends to see Lawrence Olivier in his great performance as Henry V, in the play by Shakespeare. As we were leaving the movie theater afterwards, one of our number exclaimed, "I never realized that Henry V was such a great orator!"

I reminded my friend with a smile that, after all, Shakespeare was a pretty good speech writer.

At that, she shook her head a little, in surprise, then, laughing self-deprecatingly, replied, "I guess that's right! I was so caught up in the mood of the play that I forgot all about Shakespeare."

What greater compliment could an artist receive than to be so completely believed! And yet, had Shakespeare quoted verbatim what King Henry really said, Henry's would have been the artistry, not Shakespeare's.

The balance between exactly duplicating reality, and inventing one's own reality, is an impossible one to legislate artistically. Thoughts on the subject range all the way from stark realism to steamy surrealism: from reproducing objective reality exactly as it is, to creating strange shapes and fantasies that express no objective reality at all, but only a subconscious creation, mildly stimulated, perhaps, by objective reality.

Even as impersonal a medium as the camera, however, cannot but be selective according to the consciousness of the photographer. The more selective he is, the more his work deserves to be classified as true art. And even the most surreal of painters must be objective enough to know how to touch others at some level of their inner reality, otherwise no one will buy his work. The more he knows how to touch others, the more his work, too, deserves to be classified as true art.

It comes down to the fact that we are all only small parts of a greater reality. We are influenced by that reality. And we would like to have some influence on it in return, if only in a spirit of grateful reciprocity. The arts are mankind's way of interacting, especially on a feeling level, with objective nature.

In any true interaction, there is respect for that with which, or that person with whom, one is interacting. There is receptivity to the other's realities, as well as a sensitive reply in terms of one's own realities.

Interaction is not monologue. Nor is it merely repeating the other fellow's remarks. In any artistic expression, there is always a temptation to seek one of these two extremes: passivity on the one hand, or aggressive self-affirmation on the other. Some artists abdicate all responsibility. Refusing the opportunity for interaction, they let Nature do all the talking. We might call these the Super-Realists. Other artists cloud the clarity of interaction by shouting so obstreperously that Nature never gets a chance to open her mouth. These, we might call the Super-Surrealists. True Crystal Clarity exists at neither extreme.

What is it that prevents clarity in artistic expression? In the case of the Super-Realist, it is lack of true appreciation for the artist's role. In the case of the Super-Surrealist, it is an exaggerated sense of the importance of his role. To find the middle ground between these extremes, the artist needs to work at achieving inner clarity.

The inability to appreciate one's true role as an artist can be overcome by realizing that interaction need not be conducted "out there," where his subject is, but more inwardly, in himself. The artist could concentrate on how he *feels*, when looking, say, at a field. His block to communication may lie, not so much in an inability to feel, as in a lack of clarity in seeing how feeling relates to what he is depicting.

Overreaction, at the other end of the spectrum, can be overcome, instead, by projecting the mind more outwardly toward the subject of one's study, and then "listening" to what it has to say.

Emotional reactions estrange one from objective realities, just as they often do in interactions between people. Just think of the storm of reaction, in artistic circles especially, to statements by scientists that the universe doesn't seem to be ruled by human expectations. Haven't those reactions, like a swelling tide of gossip, confused the issue more than they've clarified it?

"Science tells us that everything is meaningless!" "We are all aliens in a hostile universe!" "We are the mere playthings of an unfeeling destiny!" The reactions have continued to build up, each one feeding on those before it, reaching the point where some people have actually committed suicide in a final act of protest.

People forget that Einstein himself was a deeply spiritual man, though certainly not religious in the orthodox sense.

Emotional reactions can only confuse the picture of reality; they cannot clarify it. The alternative to reacting emotionally isn't to address every issue with cold logic: It is to tune in with calm, intuitive feeling, as opposed to agitated emotions, to whatever reality one wants to address.

Intuitive feeling, however, is difficult to achieve if one insists on allowing his personal desires to intervene.

Supposing Shakespeare, in describing Henry V's historic victory at Agincourt, had decided, "I hate war. Oh, how I wish Henry hadn't gone off to France in the first place!" Instead of making the welkin ring with the cry:

"Into the breach, dear friends,
 Or close the wall up with our English dead!"

he might have given us something like this:

"Go if you must, poor lambs,
 But, ah! the tally of our English dead!"

and the glorious victory would have looked like a virtual defeat. Shakespeare, in this case, would simply have been creating his own story — one that had nothing to do with the actual story of what happened that day on the fields of France.

A common question asked of artists in every field is, "What have you tried to say?" Sincere artists certainly prefer this question to the other one so often posed them: "Whom are you trying to reach?" But in fact, both concepts are inadequate. Creative clarity demands that personal desire be reduced to a minimum.

Here, then, is a better question for every artist to ask himself: "What is trying to be said here?" Or: "What is trying to happen here?"

The point of this less self-centered question is to reduce the ego's intrusion to a minimum, so as all the better to tune in to a larger reality. Instead of asking oneself, then, "What do I want?" one might also ask, "In order to express the mood I want, what is appropriate?" One should ask oneself, even of the mood itself, "Is it appropriate?" A children's song — to give an obvious example — must have a quality of lightness no matter how heavy one's own mood happens to be that day. If you simply can't manage to lift yourself out of that mood, better skip the song for the time being, and turn to some subject with which you do feel in tune.

An interesting phenomenon in the arts is the number of great painters, composers, and writers who have lost their sanity since the time when society began encouraging artists to develop their egos as artists. One thinks of Van Gogh, of Schumann and Hugo Wolf, of Friedrich Nietzsche. The list is dismayingly long. Madness, prior to the Romantic Movement, was no more common among artists than it was among any other class of human beings. Why is genius nowadays so often equated with insanity?

Well, certainly, an excess of energy to the nerves in any part of the body can have a damaging effect on them. Too much energy to the brain is unquestionably capable of disturbing a person's mental equilibrium. Does this mean, however, that the solution is to direct less energy to the brain? Creative genius is notable for its high energy. Genius operates, moreover, principally through the brain. Shall we say, then, that the solution is less genius, and more attention, perhaps, to one's stomach?

Fortunately not, for it isn't energy to the brain that causes the mental imbalance. It is the blockage of energy *in* the brain. This blockage occurs with any strong emphasis on the thought, "I." The energy that flows up to the brain must be released to flow onward. The same is true in the muscles of the body: It is tension, holding the energy there, that causes the damage.

Think of a freeway with only a few cars moving on it. Two cars are stopped on the side of the road, apparently having been involved in an accident.

Other cars slow down a little, partly out of concern for the safety of the people at the side of the road, and partly just out of curiosity. Because the number of cars is small, the overall flow of traffic is not affected.

Now, suppose the time is rush hour, and the freeway is crowded. Cars slow down a little at the accident, as before. Because there are so many cars now, however, the process of slowing down at the accident causes a delay on the freeway that results in stop-and-go driving even as far back as one or two miles.

The ego is an energy-stopper in creative activity of all kinds. The simple thought, "*I* am painting a tree," as opposed to, "I am painting a *tree*," is enough to hinder the clear flow of inspiration. The greater the creative flow of energy, moreover, the greater the stoppage of energy in the thought of "I." Creative artists are more apt than many people to be egotistical, not because their egos are naturally stronger, but simply because there is a greater energy-flow through the ego to the brain. It is more important for artists, therefore, than for many people to exclude the ego principle as much as possible during their creative work.

Paramhansa Yogananda, the great yogi, wrote that the seat of the ego is the medulla oblongata, at the base of the brain. It is, in fact, most interesting to note that any increase in the thought, "I," seems to produce a greater focus of energy at that point. Try it, and see if you don't find it so yourself. See what happens, for example, when you feel pleased by flattery.

The way to remove this energy block, Yogananda said, was to divert one's concentration from the medulla oblongata and focus it at what he said was the seat of concentration, in the forehead between the eyebrows. Thence, he said, one should project it outward toward whatever one is doing.

For people who have no awareness of the energy-flow in their bodies, or of blockages to that flow in the brain, it should be easy all the same to understand that the ego is more of an obstruction than an aid to artistic expression. For it is always more productive, whatever the circumstance, to think, "What is appropriate?" than, "What do *I* want in this situation?"

Does the ego play no role at all in creativity? Yes, certainly it does. The ego is, for one thing, the initiator of creativity. After the question, "What is appropriate?" moreover, it usually is faced with several choices, and must ask itself, "With which of these alternatives do I feel the most comfortable?" Thereafter, it should constantly hold up to the mind the question, "Is what I'm saying appropriate to what I've set out to say?"

The ego should keep a firm rein on the flow of thought, to make sure it doesn't get sidetracked. For there arises constantly the temptation to use what one is creating as an opportunity, for example, to show off one's skill. Among famous composers, indeed, the only one I know who didn't succumb at least occasionally to this temptation was Mozart. So true was Mozart to his musical inspiration that when his publisher wrote him that if he wouldn't write a little more in the popular vein he would starve, Mozart wrote back that in that case he had no choice but to starve.

The ego's role in creativity is, indeed, basic. The important thing only is that it join in the fun, and not ruin everything by calling all attention to itself.

True creativity is ever new, ever fresh. In its flow, when it is crystal clear, the demands of every occasion become unique, each moment, purely itself. The more vitally creative the artist, the less he thinks of drawing on past associations of thought and experience. For he lives in the *here* and *now*, seeking ever to catch those sub-currents in the tides of time which never take one in exactly the same direction twice.

To achieve Crystal Clarity in one's perceptions, another quality is essential: complete self-honesty. Self-honesty is, indeed, an excellent definition of humility. For real humility is not self-deprecation (that would only imply continued, but negative, concentration on the ego!), but the simple recognition of how little man's role is in the broader scheme of things. And isn't such recognition the fruit of complete self-honesty?

Tuning in to what is trying to happen is, to a great extent, what I mean by Crystal Clarity.

Remember, a little unclarity at the source of creativity may result in no clarity at all at the end. It is like the successive generations of a tape recording, every copy of which reduces to some extent its fidelity. High fidelity is needed in the original recording, if the tape that gets sold in the music stores is to give an acceptable idea of the beauty of the original concert. A great deal of clarity, similarly, is needed at the source of inspiration, since from that point its quality can only diminish.

Chapter Eight

Responsibility in The Arts

If there is a class of people that have a reputation for social irresponsibility (the reputation, let's face it, is not wholly undeserved), it is artists. Let us not insist, therefore, on social responsibility as our theme. But let us address, rather, the simpler question of the artist's responsibility to himself.

What does an artist want to achieve? More basically still, why do people become artists?

For one obvious reason, they want to express themselves — their feelings, their opinions, their insights. No one, probably, wants his self-expression to separate him from reality. He wants it to put him more deeply in touch at least with certain aspects of reality.

This is to say that his first responsibility, forever

self-assigned, as an artist is to express himself, not chaotically, but with a measure of purpose. Even if that purpose doesn't involve communication with anyone else, it does at least involve a hope of achieving some sort of clarification for himself, of his own feelings and ideas.

As a creative human being, moreover, he will, necessarily, be looking for some sort of development — whether outwardly as an artist, or inwardly as a human being — from his artistic expression.

Certainly, he will not want to stagnate in whatever awareness he chooses for himself. To a creative person, stagnation would be unacceptable. More likely, he will want, through his art, to clarify his awareness.

Surely, then, it is obvious that creativity cannot be divorced from purpose. Almost as inevitably, moreover, any creative person will hope to develop in some way personally by means of his creative expression.

So then, even if an artist doesn't want to communicate with anyone, he must certainly want to communicate with reality on *some* level, and in some way to gain personally by that communication.

Here is an example of a writer who wasn't aware that he had any such intention. P. G. Wodehouse, the British humorist, remarked that humanity, at his death, would be "one message short." Hillaire Belloc called him the best English writer then living, an appraisal with which I agree.

Wodehouse was a humorist, and can't have been expected to speak of his art in terms of its "deeper purpose." He *was* serious about it, however; he was serious even about the happiness that he tried, with great success, to share with others. As Joseph Connolly Hampstead put it in a tribute to him, "Behind the happy face there lurked a happy man."

To be serious about something shouldn't have to be equated with the furrowed brow, set jaw, and a surrounding nimbus of gloom. Wodehouse's wonderful creations of inspired lunacy provide a sort of "God's-eye view" of the world, one in which everything mankind does with so much self-importance appears slightly — though always in a kindly light — absurd. Wodehouse's message to humanity — though he himself never saw it as a "message" — was to view life happily, as a genuine friend and well-wisher of mankind.

Artists generally are not philosophers. The majority of them haven't the knack of verbalizing what they try to express. They would rather communicate with paintbrushes or chisels, or perhaps by humming what they have to say. What I've said, however, must be acceptable even to the artist who has never verbalized a concept — namely, that the creative artist wants to communicate with reality at some level, and through his work to deepen that communication.

This, then, is his responsibility to himself. It is self-assigned. No one else has burdened him with it.

Jesus Christ, when criticized for healing a sick person on the sabbath, gave this immortal reply, one which revealed him to be a man of perfect common sense: "The Sabbath was made for man, and not man for the Sabbath." His statement can be applied to the arts as well, with the perfectly reasonable claim: "The arts were made for man, and not man for the arts."

The oft-heard slogan, "Art for art's sake," by contrast, shows no common sense at all. Has art any conscious "sake" to be taken into consideration? It is mankind who must be considered, whenever the subject under discussion involves some human activity.

What will deepen a person's ability to relate to, or communicate with, reality at any level is, simply, *Crystal Clarity*. Communication never springs out of bewilderment, nor out of muddy, confused thinking or feeling. It is the result of clarity. Clarity, indeed, is almost an end to be sought in itself. For with progressive clarity alone comes the dawn of increasing understanding.

The artist has a further responsibility to himself: his own mental well-being. No one, surely, wants to deepen whatever suffering he feels. When an artist, through his art, cries out in grief or anger, he can only be doing so in the belief that, by expressing his emotions, he will gain some relief from them.

It is a simple fact of life that everyone, without exception, wants to banish pain from his life, and to find happiness.

Clarity, as I said in the last chapter, expands one's vision of reality, and in the process creates a more positive outlook on life.

There is another vitally important aspect to the matter: *One is influenced by whatever state of consciousness he invites to flow through him.*

If he decides to write, or paint, or express himself artistically in any way, he should know that negative self-expression will not relieve him of his negative feelings; it will only deepen them. The expression of darkness cannot but generate more darkness in the person who expresses it. The expression of light brings light into the life of the person who offers himself as a channel for the light. Darkness breeds sorrow, and suffering, and despair. Light inspires understanding, acceptance, and joy. Is the choice between these two really so difficult to make?

The artist's responsibility to himself is to express things that are worthwhile. This is not to say that they must be worthwhile in the world's eyes. They must certainly be so, however — and with ever-increasing clarity — in his own.

Many artists, as I said earlier, feel that they have no need to express themselves meaningfully to others. Yet I wonder if this is really so. Those same artists are seldom above trying to shock their more staid and pompous fellow citizens. As the French poet, Baudelaire, put it, *"Il faut épater le bourgeois"* ("One must shock the bourgeois"). Isn't this very desire to shock an indication that, on some level of their consciousness, they have a desire to teach? What else is implied in wanting to teach them a lesson? Obviously, their desire is both to express themselves meaningfully and to communicate — even if they themselves are not aware of this second motive.

It is simply not possible for artists to get away from expressing some sort of meaning through their art. The very cry of so many of them that life is meaningless is, in its own way, intended as a meaningful statement.

In the last analysis, indeed, we are all human beings first. Whatever we do with our lives, outwardly, is only secondary. It is with human values that artists, along with all the rest of us, have to learn to cope.

Every artist, then, would do well in the very name of self-responsibility and self-fulfillment to express true, as opposed to false, meanings in his art. This is the same thing, as we have already seen, as saying that he should do his best to express Crystal Clarity, not confusion, both in his art and in his life.

The artist may reject the need for inspiring others. He would be foolish, however, to reject the need for discovering more inspiration in his own life.

This thought alone should be his incentive for communicating with others through his art. For it is a simple fact of human life that one finds more personal inspiration, and thereby greater personal fulfillment, if he tries to share with others.

Any attempt at communication with others, moreover, helps the artist in another way also, once he understands the vital need to achieve personal clarity for himself. For it often happens that, when we communicate our feelings and ideas to others, in the very process of trying to clarify them we find them becoming clearer to us. Sincere communication with others helps one to bring out into the open thoughts and impressions that, until then, may have been vague in his own mind.

In offering the fruits of one's artistic labors to others, finally, one finds one of the best ways for removing the blockage of ego in oneself. This, too, is a motive for creating a genre of art that seems some-

times almost to have been forgotten: works that can
be cherished, rather than merely endured.

Chapter Nine

Crystal Clarity: A New Concept

It is generally accepted that the arts have the ability to "say something," even if the work is an abstract painting, or an unnamed musical "étude." Often it is said that music, for example, is a "universal language," inasmuch as a piece of music composed by a Frenchman or an American might be enjoyed as much in Bangkok or Bombay as in Paris or New York.

What is it, however, specifically, that can be said through the arts? This is something not so generally known. I don't believe the subject has ever been taught in school. Artists themselves, even the greatest of them, have been more concerned with describing technical matters like symmetry, color balance, chord progression, alliteration, and the like than with discussing the relationship between any of these outward factors and human consciousness. I know of no system that emphasizes this relationship. And I've often wondered how is it that something so obvious should have been overlooked?

If, as everyone claims, the arts are a form of language, then there can be no doubt that they are seen already as a means of communication. So, then — what is it that they communicate?

Is the only way to make any sort of meaningful statement through the arts to be totally graphic? Must one create something like Diego Rivera's bold visual appeals for social justice to the worker and the downtrodden masses, if one wants to say something meaningful about suffering? Must one twist a piece of welded metal around upon itself and label it "Soul in Torment" to be understood? Must the ballet dancer drop the ballerina he's been holding aloft (I've often rather wished he would!), to convey the symbol of disappointed aspiration? In short, must one be obvious, even blatant, if he wants to *say* anything at all?

Small wonder so many artists, in their rejection of social causes, seek "meaning" in such things as color shading, or in the "tension between their conceptual approach to construction and the associational power of the objects they assemble." But they are abdicating their responsibility at a time when meaning vs. meaninglessness has become a crucial issue.

Back in the days of Rafael, Leonardo, Botticelli, and Michelangelo, the question of meaning was not an issue. Those artists depicted scenes, or people, usually from the Bible or from the recognized classical themes of ancient Greece. In music, too, perceptions were more literal than they are today. The composer Gluck, in his preface to *Alceste*, wrote: "I have striven to restrict music to its true office of serving poetry by means of expression and by following the situations of the story."

Nowadays, there is a need to identify meaning more subtly. Nor in this case does it mean we have fallen from a previous ideal (as we have done, for example, in giving so much emphasis to the artist's ego). In a world where matter itself is known to be only energy, form and substance assume less importance. It is what lies *behind* the form and substance that invites attention.

Things, in former times, were considered merely inert. Now, they are seen as vibrations.

Two chapters ago, I discussed an artist's need to ask himself, "What is trying to express itself here?" Two centuries ago — even, perhaps, two decades ago — such a question couldn't have been so much as suggested in a book. Imagine someone wrestling with this sort of concept in the Eighteenth Century's "Age of Reason," or at the height of Nineteen Century materialism.

Samuel Johnson's answer to Bishop Berkeley's claim that everything exists only in thought was to give Boswell a sound kick in the seat of the trousers and ask this faithful sidekick of his whether the pain of it was only an idea in his mind. That's all it was, of course, but how many in those days were prepared to understand it as such? The thought that any mere *thing* could be "trying to express itself" would have seemed ludicrous. But nowadays?

Nowadays, realizing that material objects exist as vibrations, we find it easier to understand everything in vibratory terms. Indeed, why *shouldn't* places have vibrations as well? They do, as anyone can attest who has tried to sense intuitively the places he has visited, instead of merely observing them with his Baedeker in hand. And why *shouldn't* ideas have vibrations? They do. Ideas, primarily, are what one senses in the vibrations of places. One senses the consciousness with which those places have been impregnated by people.

The question, therefore, "What is trying to happen here?" implies that there are currents of thought and consciousness around us to which we can attune ourselves, and in the process find more support for our energies than if we worked against those currents.

There is another vital point here, namely, that consciousness is expressed through matter, *and that its quality is therefore revealed in the sorts of expressions it takes.* This fact is obvious with the language of human speech. It is less so in the languages of the arts.

When a person speaks, he not only gives utterance to his ideas through words, those symbols which man has evolved to facilitate intelligent communication. He also uses melodic patterns while talking.

Certain rising notes suggest a sense of inquiry, of expectation or hope. Certain descending notes indicate disappointment, sorrow, or — depending on various factors — determination.

Emphasis on consonants indicates will power. Emphasis on the vowels indicates emotional feeling. Nasal speech often indicates pride, or an attempt by the speaker mentally to remove himself (perhaps not in pride, but only in a spirit of politeness) from his environment. The tone of a person's voice can indicate kindness, love, irritation, anger, or enthusiasm — all of these, feelings that are instantly conveyed to the listener.

Very obviously, consciousness does express itself through the human voice, and not only through the words we use.

So far, however, no one seems to have studied non-verbal communication as a language in its own right, that is to say, as a vehicle of communication.

I myself have studied this phenomenon during more than forty years of traveling around the world. I have become convinced that in this direction lies the next step in our culture's artistic development.

For the problem presently before us is how to lift the arts out of their mire of meaninglessness and private vision, into which modern thought has caused them to stumble, but in the process not to revert to the conventions of by-gone centuries, when the opportunities for such subtlety of insight as man now possesses did not exist.

Several years ago, as I mentioned earlier, I went to the Holy Land. In each of the sacred shrines there, I sat silently and tried to *feel* what it had to say to me. What I felt in many of those places was deep. It was, moreover, specific to each place, and different from all the others. In some of the shrines I felt an enormous blessing; in others, a more human consciousness. Always, however, where I experienced anything at all, the feeling was specific.

From Israel I returned to Italy, where I stayed for a month or so in Sorrento. There, removed from the actual scenes and restless activity of traveling, I sat down to relive in my mind what I had experienced in Israel. When the memory of the feeling associated with each place was clear in my mind, I held that feeling up to the inner silence, with this loving demand: "Translate what I am feeling into the language of music." Instantly, in each case, a melody came to me. And in each case, it perfectly expressed the feeling. I was amazed at how perfectly the music for the Holy Sepulchre, for example, expressed the blessing I'd experienced there.

Twenty of these melodies came to me in a single day. Later, after I'd arranged and recorded them, I combined them with color slides that I'd taken, to form a multi-media presentation that I called, **Christ Lives in the Holy Land**. The response to this presentation everywhere has been deeply gratifying.

An elderly lady said to me after one evening's performance, "In all my sixty-five years, this is the most inspiring evening I've ever experienced!" I was more moved than I can say when, having thanked me, she genuflected. Her gratitude was not to me. It was not even to the music, but rather to the inspiration she had felt coming to her *through* the music. And at that level of reality, I, too, shared, and still share, her gratitude.

There have been other times, however, when I felt no particular vibrations in a place for which I hoped to write a piece of music. In such cases what I've found works for me is to project onto that place feelings that seem to me compatible with the environment. I've crystalized those feelings, so to speak, giving them a clear definition in my own mind. Then, as before, I've asked the inner silence to give me a melody.

If my mental definition was sufficiently clear, the melody has come, usually instantly, and has seemed completely appropriate not only to me, but to others who had visited those places with me.

If, on the other hand, the melody wouldn't come to me, then instead of worrying at it from the musical end, I would work at clarifying my mental image. Once the image has been crystal clear, the melody has come of itself.

I have never known this method to fail. It is why I insist with so much faith that one *can* tune in, artistically, to the reality to which one wants to relate, whatever that reality, and then give it meaningful expression.

This is why I offer *Crystal Clarity* as a new concept in the arts — not merely for deeper artistic appreciation, but to offer to creative artists a means of achieving more meaningful and expansive expression through their arts.

I said in an earlier chapter that no mere technique of artistry could ever convey any feelings that may have come to be associated with that technique. A certain curve to a line in a painting, for example, might succeed in conveying a sense of joy. No automatic repetition of that curve, however, could ever duplicate the joy, any more than words alone, without feeling, could ever convey the feelings they have been known to communicate, when uttered sincerely.

Nevertheless, it may serve to give my point greater clarity, were I to share a few of the insights that have come to me during my years of study of this subject.

I noticed once, when arranging the piano accompaniment for a song, that, whereas musical convention would have demanded that the last note descend, the feeling that that descent would have given would have been a sinking downward, as if into sleep. What I wanted was a rising feeling, an upward soaring into the peace of a joyful, not a passive, state of rest. Taking just one note upward at the end of the song made this polar difference in the mood of the music.

Consider the matter of color. Don't bright, pure hues suggest more spiritual states of awareness than muddy hues? Can you imagine Leonardo's *Last Supper* done in dark, heavy tones? He could have done so only if he'd wanted to convey a deep sense of suffering, and not the divine inspiration of the Eucharist.

Dark values in Leonardo's spiritual paintings serve only to emphasize the central figures. In a sensual or violent painting, however, the muddy quality is predominant.

Different colors of themselves suggest also different states of mind. Blue, for instance, is more soothing than red. Orange is more energetic than green.

Consider lines. Short, straight lines and sharp

angles, if used sparingly, suggest will power; if used indiscriminately, tension. Curves imply harmony, adaptability, rest. A multiplicity of sharp angles suggests tension bordering on nervousness. Curves that are softened in their outlines connote almost a meditative peace.

Putting it another way, we may say that straight lines represent *doing*, whereas curved lines and circles represent *being*.

I was interested, on a visit years ago to Chandigarh, India, the architecture of which was designed by the French architect, Le Corbusier, to note how out of place those straight, Western-inspired lines seemed, rising up as they do out of timeless plains.

Curves are a more natural architectural expression of India's culture. They suggest a national consciousness that, over countless centuries, has become smoothed and rounded like the pebbles on a river bed, adapting instinctively to the universe and to life's vicissitudes. Straight lines and sharp angles, more natural to Western culture, suggest Western man's determination to conquer nature — to bend her laws to his will.

Consider tempo in music. Who has not felt the exciting influence of fast music, or been soothed by a slow, measured beat? Musical tempo is related in our subconscious to the heartbeat, which naturally speeds up under the stress of emotional excitement, and slows down when one is relaxed and peaceful. Both tempo and heartbeat are as capable of affecting the emotions as of being affected by them.

Consider rhythm. The first beat of a musical measure represents the sense of "I." If heavily affirmed, this beat implies a forceful ego. But if lightly affirmed, the spirit of the listener receives the message to rise and fly.

If the first beat is affirmed slowly and repeatedly, without deviation, one begins to feel oneself treading sedately through life, impervious to the feelings and opinions of others. Haydn's music is an example of this sort of mood. Despite his genius, many people consider him a bit of a stuffed shirt.

The first beat, when affirmed slowly, repeatedly, and *heavily*, suggests an ego so firm in its own convictions that it is prepared to march roughshod over everyone who opposes it. Hence military bands, John Philip Souza, and the whole gamut of martial music. Hence also the kind of hypnosis that has been known to seize an army when marching under the drumbeats of this kind of music, causing the soldiers to march unafraid into heavy fire.

Affirmed repeatedly but more rapidly, a highly suggestible ego can be lifted into a hysterical rhythm that is not naturally its own, and can even be induced to behave in a manner contrary to what it would accept normally.

If the first beat is virtually suspended for whole measures at a time, as it often is in the Indian classical *raga*, melody and accompanying rhythm temporarily going their separate ways, the resultant diversion from self-consciousness can have the effect of reemphasizing it again on a higher, soul-level once the original beat is at last resumed.

The other beats in a measure, being subordinate to the first, take their basic direction from it. They reveal the *quality* of the ego's drive, enthusiasm, or initiative. Six-eight time, for example, is more graceful; four-four time, more determined.

Rhythmic deviations, if held in control by the first beat, may suggest a "cool," uncommitted ego. Such a person is always surprising others, generally not from a wish to entertain them, but rather because he doesn't feel bound by their expectations of him. If the syncopation is kept light, it can suggest a joyous sense of inner freedom. But if heavy, and particularly if coupled with a heavy downbeat, the implied lack of commitment may also connote contempt for, or indifference to, the needs of others.

What one gives out to the world, however, will be received by him again in return. If one is too much interested in dishing out surprises, for example, he may end up himself being surprised. Syncopation in music can be increased to the point where it suggests unexpected events being inflicted *upon* the ego, rather than by it. "Jagged" rhythms, rhythms in which the first beat — that is to say, the ego — no longer seems in control, betray nervousness and insecurity: an ego threatened by an unpredictable and hostile universe. This influence we find in a great deal of modern music, symptomatic as it is of a restless and disoriented age.

Consider harmony. Chords generally imply human relationships. Loud, full chords give the impression of a crowd of people. Soft chords suggest more a subjective relationship with others. And in small orchestras of four or five instruments the effect may be wholly subjective, implying a relationship rather of different aspects of one personality.

Undeviating harmony suggests relationships

that are bland to the point of becoming boring. Occasional discords, crying for resolution in harmony, suggest those challenges and superficial differences which add delight to any human relationship. A continuous succession of discords, however, suggests only friction and disharmony.

Modern music lays considerable emphasis on dissonance, just as it does on syncopation. In this fact, too, is revealed an age out of harmony with itself.

Consider melody. The melodic line in a piece of music represents inner aspirations, and, in addition, one's reactions to the objective world. A rising sequence of notes tends to lift the consciousness; a sinking sequence, to lower it — though perhaps only in firmness of affirmation, not necessarily in sorrow.

Sub-melodies represent secondary, and often hidden, yearnings and desires in the personality.

High notes in the melody, coupled with a heavy downbeat, suggest an idealistic ego. (Note this effect in Beethoven's famous "Ode to Joy," from his Ninth Symphony.) Even in a high or rising melodic sequence, however, if dominated in the accompaniment by low notes, and particularly if the downbeat is heavy (here, rock music springs to mind), the impression conveyed is sensual or otherwise heavily physical.

Again, the complete lack of a melodic line — another feature of much modern "classical" music — suggests want of aspiration or ideals: an inner self adrift on an ocean without a shore.

It is interesting that Indian devotional music — the most sophisticated music that evolved in the

East — though highly melodic, is devoid of both harmony and sub-melodies. Western religious music, with its intricate melodic and harmonic patterns, is considerably richer. The statements are simply different.

Richness is something the Indian tradition seeks to avoid, owing to its stress on personal, *inner* communion with God. Western religious music is usually associated with communal worship. It may also suggest the crosscurrents of yearning that make up the complexities of the human personality. Indian religious tradition, by contrast, ignores the human personality more or less completely, and concentrates on the soul's eternal longing for its divine Source in God. Through music, the Indian worshiper is taught to seek attunement ultimately with *Aum*, the Sound of the Infinite.

The two traditions are different. Inevitably, therefore, the music that sprang out of them is different also. Each reflects the basic attitudes of its own culture.

In one of the songs I wrote for the *Christ Lives* oratorio, I wanted to express the indomitable spirit of modern Israel. Holding this thought clearly in my mind as I composed both the words and the music, it was inevitable that they should have come out forcefully. The very emphasis on consonants in the words suggests courage. Here is the song:

A New Tomorrow

When the dawn breaks, and then the morning

Sends the sun high in the sky:
Who would hide from heaven's glory?
Who would pass the challenge by?

There's a morning for every nation
When the sun's high in the sky:
There's a time for every people
To affirm their destiny.

Even so, all of us together
Can create a better land:
Leave the past! A new tomorrow
Waits for all who understand.

The important thing at all times, when expressing oneself artistically, is to hold mentally before oneself the thought, or feeling, that one is trying to express. He should refer back again and again to this concept as he progresses.

Crystal Clarity, in its present definition, is a new concept, and one that cannot but bring new life and meaning to artistic creativity. One of the principal benefits of this concept is that it reflects back on the artist, for it gives him a greater sense of meaning in his life, a more dynamic state of inner awareness, and a deeper sense of his own value as a human being.

Chapter Ten

Crystal Clarity Defined

Artistic creativity may be said to be ninety percent art, and only ten percent science. A student in art school, or at the music conservatory, may learn all the techniques there are to be learned without ever becoming thereby a true artist. Another student may receive no formal training at all, but work out his techniques slowly, through a process of trial and error. But if he is inspired from within, his inspiration will manifest itself even during the crude beginnings of his artistic career.

The technical aspects of Crystal Clarity, therefore, that I mentioned in the foregoing chapter, are insufficient to define this concept. No one, for example, could create a stirring military march merely by telling himself, "Now, I must heavily emphasize

the first beat of every measure." Conceivably, perhaps — though I myself fail to conceive it — someone clever enough might even find a way of composing a military march with an ethereal first beat,
just to show it could be done.

The real point is that inspiration cannot be ap-
proached from outside. Its wellsprings lie within.
Technique is a filter though which inspiration must
express itself, even as words are the filter through
which we express our ideas. Words, however, without inner meaning, are (to quote Shakespeare), "full
of sound and fury, signifying nothing."

Suppose, then, that two painters sit down to
paint a perfectly ordinary scene: a flowing brook, let
us say, with tall grasses growing on its banks, and a
weeping willow trailing long tendrils over the water. Let us say that both artists belong to the same
artistic tradition: realism, impressionism, cubism,
surrealism — it doesn't particularly matter which,
since schools primarily involve only the technical
side of expression. One of these artists, however,
lives by the principles of Crystal Clarity.

How will their work differ?

Let us assume they have equal technical skill, so
that the difference is on one level only. This difference, then, will be that the one who tries to make his
work an expression of Crystal Clarity will add the
fresh dimension of his own awareness. He will
strive to make the scene he depicts expressive of
something that he feels in himself while looking at
it. This he can do by framing it appropriately (if he
is a realist), or by concentrating on the lighting (if he
is an impressionist), or by projecting onto the scene

thought forms that are purely his own (if he is a surrealist). In any case, he will try to relate what he sees to some state of his own consciousness.

A Japanese artist or Haiku poet tries to get you to sense, from the few lines or from the brief word picture he gives you, a surrounding reality at which his work merely hints: a lake, perhaps, suggested to the mind by the outward curve of a few tall reeds rising out of a slanted line, with a simple, straight line below them. This kind of art is as important for the unstated reality surrounding it as for the reality it actually states.

A great artist, however, whether Japanese or-Western, will see that unstated reality as something more than esthetic. He will do more than suggest a lake: His suggestion will also be of some state of consciousness.

When an artist expresses Crystal Clarity in his art, his emphasis, similarly, will be on what is sensed beyond the reality actually seen. On the clarity of what is sensed inwardly — and also, of course, on the artist's technical proficiency — will depend the success of his painting. If the inner feelings are heavy or clouded, there can be no clarity in them, but only confusion. Such a painting, then, will never be able to express true clarity.

Creativity may be equated with originality only when originality is not, in its turn, defined as unpredictability. Originality of expression must be understood, rather, as an expression that *originates* from within a person, from his sincere inner feelings, rather than from an attempt to react to something whose origins lie outside of him.

"I love you" can become a platitude the very first time it is repeated, if when one repeats it the meaning of the words is not deeply felt. Sincerely stated, however, do the words ever pall?

Monet painted virtually the same water lilies hundreds of times. His love for them, however, remained ever fresh. And that is why one never tires of seeing them.

The relationship between a thing seen and the consciousness one experiences on seeing it cannot be a mental perception only. It must come from inner clarity, which involves one on deeper levels. The more *clearly* one's whole being enters into the experience, the more crystal clear will be his expression of it.

There is a company in Germany that sells slide shows of a pilgrimage to the Holy Land. The photographer obviously went to great lengths, in the name of originality, to get shots that were "different." One scene, for example, is of Mt. Tabor, the Mount of Transfiguration, taken from above. I am impressed by the expense he must have incurred in hiring a helicopter with the sole purpose of shooting that one picture. And I can imagine his self-congratulation, thinking, "There, now! Who else ever thought to capture the mountain from *this* angle?"

And so the mountain in his view of it looks short, squat, and a bit silly. The color slide offers not the slightest suggestion of the great drama with which that mountain is historically associated.

The photographer took another shot — if memory serves, in fact, a sequence of them — of pilgrims in procession on the Via Dolorosa, the route Jesus walked on his way to be crucified. Again, in a smug effort to be different — or "original" — the photographer climbed up onto a housetop and photographed the whole scene from above. What he got were fat little figures that looked more comical than emotionally involved in the tragedy of the event they were reliving.

Originality ought not to be equated with novelty. Unfortunately, many people confuse the two. I don't even claim novelty for the concept "Crystal Clarity," except in the sense of bringing certain timeless truths more clearly into focus for modern times.

Photography happens to be a hobby of mine. In Hawaii, several years ago, I took many shots of flowers and scenery. I therefore found myself noticing more particularly the quality of photographs that I found on display in galleries and card shops.

The more of these photographs I studied, the more it amazed me to see how few of the photographers had given the slightest thought to any kind of meaningful relationship to their subjects. A few had tried to be original, but this was "originality" in mere competition with other people's "originality." None of it came from within.

There was a photograph of a bird of paradise — a tropical flower which, when fully open, resembles an exotic bird in flight. Half open, however, the flower looks like nothing at all — a sort of "ugly duckling" that hasn't yet turned into a swan. And that is how the photographer had chosen to photograph the flower. One can imagine his pride in his "originality"!

The bird of paradise is a flower that evokes thoughts of lush, tropical greenery; perhaps of a simple, untroubled life in harmonious surroundings; perhaps, indeed, of some heaven. Deep shades of green are, in fact, its natural background. So what did one photographer do, just to be different? He photographed one of these flowers against a beige soil background. He hadn't even created an interesting contrast in the colors, as he'd have wanted to do had he been striving for something other than beauty: shock value, for example. Let's face it, however; he *was* different!

Another photograph I saw was of a bed of delicate flowers massed sprawlingly together on a hillside, so that, instead of giving emphasis to their delicacy, it presented only a confusion of white.

Photography is perhaps the best medium for illustrating what I mean by Crystal Clarity, for unless one goes to pains to select his scene with attention to something he wants to express, the resulting photograph won't show any influence of conscious involvement at all. He will be like those hordes of Japanese tourists one sees, smiling as they pose for photographs before the Parthenon or the Taj Mahal, but with no more interest in the picture than to say to the folks back home, "See? I was there!"

Back, then, to our two painters by the brook. The one who tries to express the principles of Crystal Clarity, if he is perceptive, won't mentally review what others have done and try to be "different." He won't think, "Now, what state of awareness shall we try to express today? Let me see — joy? misery? rising hope? abject despair?" Any such playing with ideas, instead of sensitively tuning in to a true experience, cannot result in clarity of any kind, except perhaps intellectual. And intellectual art is nearly always stillborn.

A perceptive artist will reach out mental tendrils, let us say, to the tendrils of the weeping willow, and ask them, "What have we to say to each other?" He will enter into a kind of soul-conversation with the tree, the brook, the grassy bank. There will be, on his side anyway, a sense of actual communication with his subject, not of mere projection on his part.

If nothing else, what endeavoring to paint from a sense of Crystal Clarity will give him is an opening *within himself* of fresh, *and ever fresher*, levels of awareness. As he looks upon the world with this attitude, he will begin to find himself living in more conscious, clearer, and (to him) more meaningful relationship to everything and everyone. At least this much will be accomplished, and this is already a great deal.

There is, however, a further, and fascinating, possibility. For by seeking to communicate consciously with the world around us, we may be doing more than developing our sensitive awareness. The world, too, may have the capacity to respond in some way.

This may seem a fantastic notion. Consider, however, this line of reasoning, and see if it doesn't hold promise.

Science has erased the dividing line between organic and inorganic matter. Organic matter, it is now known, can show all the properties of inorganic matter. From this discovery, modern writers have drawn the conclusion that organic matter is essentially inanimate, that even human consciousness is simply the electronic "manipulation of memory traces in the brain" — that we are, in fact, nothing more than biologically produced computers.

As a communist torturer is reported once to have said to his victim, a young girl in her teens, "What does your suffering have to do with me? You are actually no more conscious than that wall over there." Such, indeed, is the only logical natural outcome of a wholly materialistic view of reality: Values don't exist. People don't matter. The only thing that may matter is ordering their existence in the most mechanically efficient way possible.

In philosophical inquiry, as in any scientific investigation, it is important to pursue avenues of thought that open up onto the broadest possible vistas, instead of those that lead to a dead end. Materialism is not only a sterile view of things: It leads into a cul-de-sac from which there is no exit, except to go back the way one came.

There is another perfectly reasonable and infinitely more promising explanation for the nature of material reality: Instead of concluding from the similarities between organic and inorganic matter that all things are essentially inanimate, to conclude from the same data that inanimate matter is really animate also, and that there is consciousness in everything.

There have been a number of experiments with plants that demonstrate their response to human thoughts. In response to thoughts of love, they have been found to flourish, whereas thoughts of hatred have made them wilt and die — even when all other treatment (sunshine, watering schedule, etc.) was the same.

After a showing of color slides that I'd taken in Hawaii, one lady from the audience came up to me and remarked, "I got the feeling that the flowers in your pictures were responding to your love for them." Was this merely a pretty fancy?

The possibilities, at any rate for the artist, inherent in an actual two-way communication with his subject are endlessly intriguing. One wonders whether it has not existed often, even without the artist's conscious awareness.

Perhaps those lively flowers of Van Gogh's actually looked as lively as he painted them because they were reflecting back to him the life he was giving out to them!

In a more obviously acceptable instance, maybe the sour faces on so many classical portraits were the result of the artist taking energy from his subject, but giving out none in return.

On the basis of everything that I've written so far on the subject, let me now offer a definition of Crystal Clarity:

Crystal Clarity means to see oneself, and all things, as aspects of a greater reality; to seek to enter into conscious attunement with that reality; and to see all things as channels for the expression of that reality.

It means to see truth in simplicity; to seek always to be guided by the simple truth, not by opinion, and by what *is*, not by one's own desires or

prejudices.

It means striving to see things in relation to their broadest potential.

In one's association with other people, it means seeking always to include their realities in one's own.

What this definition does, necessarily, and apart from all merely artistic considerations, is bring artistic expression back where it belongs: to an expression of human, and not merely esthetic, values. The arts, as I said earlier, were made for man, not man for the arts.

In view of the essential human merit of artistic experience, the last chapters of this book will propose a few guidelines that might be followed by creative artists in every field in their efforts to bring inner clarity to a level where it may be called *crystalline*.

For crystals, it may be pointed out, are essentially *transmitters* of beauty. They do not produce beauty in isolation, but only in interaction with their environment. They may enhance whatever beauty they receive, but even this enhancement is reciprocal with their environment. The clearer the crystal, the more clearly it transmits whatever it receives.

I invite my readers to investigate the vast opportunities inherent in approaching the arts with Crystal Clarity. May the arts, thus, become clear channels for that great reality of which they, like all human expressions, are but a part.

Chapter Eleven

Energy in the Arts

The *sine qua non* of greatness in every form, whether artistic or human, is *energy*.

Thomas Edison claimed that genius is "one percent inspiration and ninety-nine percent perspiration." Another famous definition of genius was this one by Jane Ellice Hopkins: "Genius is an infinite capacity for taking pains."

With due deference to both these famous definitions, however, it seems to me they both fail to convey the truth intended. Many great works have been born, not laboriously or with pain and perspiration, but quickly and easily. It was almost as if they created themselves.

Franz Schubert wrote eight of his best songs in a single afternoon. Shakespeare is said to have tossed off his comedies almost carelessly.*

On the other hand, I remember reading in the newspaper about an immigrant to America who had wanted to give suitable expression to his gratitude to this country for allowing him to settle here. For twenty-five years he had labored zealously to create, out of match sticks, a huge replica of the Statue of Liberty. The resulting monstrosity was proof as pathetic, surely, as anyone ever gave of the relative unimportance of perspiration in the formula for genius.

Energy, not drudgery, is the true key to greatness. Edison might justifiably have given energy 100% of the credit. For a strong flow of energy, like the flow of electricity in a copper wire, creates a magnetic field that actually attracts inspiration to itself. A great amount of energy applied to problems may bring speedy solutions where low-keyed deliberations will always, even after laborious months, end in bathos or in half-hearted compromise.

Great works invariably proceed from great resources of energy. Sometimes it is necessary to apply this energy painstakingly. One's co-workers, if any, may even abandon the job in exhaustion or despair. Genius therefore may well involve "perspiration." But the same energy may also achieve re-

---

*Careless sometimes he most certainly was. Consider the shockingly casual way, in the final scene of *As You Like It*, that he fairly washes his hands of the story. Realizing that he must somehow dispose of the villain, Duke Frederick, who was last reported advancing with an army, he offers us the totally unexpected, in fact incredible, report of the duke's sudden conversion and withdrawal into a monastery. This is, I think, the most improbable religious conversion in all of literature.

sults with such lightning speed that everyone is left gasping for breath. In any case, the strength of the energy-flow, not the doggedness of one's perseverance, is what determines the quality of the results.

A strong flow of energy can be vividly sensed in all great works of art. They carry an almost tangible aura of vitality. On the other hand, vitality is the one thing most conspicuously lacking in minor works.

In a minor novel, the villain seems merely unattractive; the hero, merely less unattractive than the villain. The professor, if there is one, impresses the reader as nothing but a tiresome pedant. If a rustic adorns the tale, he is so convincingly dull as to be simply uninteresting. Ennui wafts though the pages of such books like marsh gasses on a tired breeze. And facts — a plenitude of them — are generally offered in desperate compensation for an utter dearth of insights, of vital reactions and observations.

In a work of true clarity, however, even far-from-edifying characters somehow charm us, or thrill us with their mysterious power. The villainy of Shakespeare's Iago suggests almost a primal force. The pedantry of Polonius is a sheer delight; at the same time, it is unexpectedly wise. Caliban's loutishness, in *The Tempest*, qualifies him as a veritable king of louts. And the ineptitude of Bottom, the weaver, in *A Midsummer Night's Dream*, is from start to finish inspired.

Energy is the redeeming quality in the works of many lesser men, too. Francois Villon, thief and notorious troublemaker though he was, wrote peotry of such intensity that it is still counted among the best literary products of his age.

In every case, it is *energy* that makes possible vital expression in the arts. Energy is the starting point of greatness, and the ladder by which every successive stage to greatness is achieved.

Chapter Twelve

Seeing Underlying Relationships

On the surface of our lives, how different we all seem from one another! Fishermen, shopkeepers, doctors, lawyers, factory workers, housewives; Americans, Chinese, Frenchmen; rich, poor, energetic, lazy: The variety is endless. No two thumbprints are exactly alike. It is man's most primitive instinct, bound as he is by ego-consciousness, to distinguish between himself and others, and then to emphasize the differences.

His sense of kinship with his fellow creatures usually evolves out of much suffering. For suffering helps to erode the thick walls of egotism.

The vision of unity in apparent diversity is common to those of clear insight. It is a vision, however, toward which one grows only by gradual degrees of inner refinement. It cannot proceed from any mere shift in opinions or in one's philosophy.

And that unitive vision is valid. For such is the nature of things that, behind their mask of separateness, differences disappear. All living beings, all things, all thoughts, all emotions and inspirations are like waves on an ocean, endlessly varied, yet forever manifestations of a single reality.

This is the vision that science has shown us of matter. It is the vision that the Scriptures have given us of life. And it is the vision artists achieve who truly understand their fellowman.

For understanding comes more by empathy than by cold analysis. Only by genuine kindness can we really get to know one another. Thus, in the hands of a true friend of humanity like Shakespeare, even a villainous Shylock seems at last pathetic also, as though, given just the right circumstances, any one of us might have fallen into the trap of his delusions.

Indeed, a dramatist of Shakespeare's stature makes the more sensitive members of his audiences feel that, in Shylock's fall, they too have fallen, in a sense. For the life in them is also that which gives birth to people like Shylock. In our deepest reality, we *are* Shylock, and Shylock is each one of us.

For no man exists who does not contain within himself the potentials of all other men.

Crystal Clarity in the arts, then, as also in human awareness, involves an ever-clearer perception of underlying relationships between dissimilar-seeming people, places, and circumstances. Its vision is always unitive.

Chapter Thirteen

Expansive Vision

The vision of people of clear insight is always expansive. Its perceptions always hint at broader realities.

A merely gifted composer, but not a truly perceptive one, in struggling to capture in music the mood of a moonrise, will tend to dwell on the uniqueness of what he sees. If he can distinguish between this evening and all others, he will do so. If he can find a way to demonstrate his own extraordinary sensitivity to this unique occasion, he will not waste the opportunity. Probably it won't even occur to him to see in the moonrise a symbol of abstract principles (hope, for example, or purity), or of universal facts of nature like the whirling of countless stars and galaxies through infinite space.

A composer, on the other hand, who is blessed with that vision which we equate with greatness, will instinctively link the moonrise to a broader drama of space, time, and being. In depicting his own reaction to the event, he will seek instinctively to express the reaction of mankind, not of his own limited personality, with its particular likes and dislikes. Probably he won't even be conscious of his own likes and dislikes while viewing such a scene.

Art that is crystal clear, while never sacrificing its awareness of the particular, scans the finest details of that particular for windows onto infinity. The expansive tendency of such art is reflected in these glorious lines on the dawn, from the *Rig Veda*:

> Last of innumerable dawns gone by,
> First of endless dawns still to come.

It is reflected in William Blake's "Auguries of Innocence," in what are probably his most famous lines:

> To see a World in a Grain of Sand
> And a Heaven in a Wild Flower,
> Hold Infinity in the palm of your hand
> And Eternity in an hour.

Great art is always, whether deliberately or by some sure instinct, a living embodiment of this principle, for the simple reason that expansiveness is instinctive to the consciousness of every great human being. Greatness, indeed, *means* a greater-than-normal vision of reality — an awareness of the whole even while concentrating on the part — as opposed to smallness in human nature, which thinks only of the part even while viewing the whole.

The less a work of art expresses the quality of Crystal Clarity, the more it becomes directed toward the particular. And the more it expresses this quality, the more it is directed expansively from the particular to the universal.

Chapter Fourteen

"Facing the Darkness"

Some years ago I was invited to lecture before a community that was dedicated to practicing the principles of Carl Jung. The members believed in "facing the darkness" in themselves. They strove for total self-honesty with respect to their human tendency to rationalize their inner faults and weaknesses. They sifted through their dreams every morning in search of deeper insight into their subconscious desires and frustrations, which they felt kept them from being the free spirits they wanted to become.

In principle, certainly, what they were striving for was admirable. We'll never achieve freedom from all our inner demons so long as we don't even know they're there, or haven't the courage to face them once we accept their existence. Without complete self-honesty, no one can grow in truth.

I've often listened with misgiving, however, to expositions of this philosophy. First of all — and this is one of the problems with a great deal of modern psychology — merely to recognize a problem intellectually, and even to face it bravely on an intellectual level, isn't at all the same thing as overcoming it. The more intelligent the person, indeed, the greater the pleasure he may take in exposing to himself and others the intricacy of his mental rationalizations.

I've listened to such people hold forth at length, all the while smiling at the subtlety of their own insight, on the subject of their own "inner darknesses." And then I've asked myself, "With all this self-exposure, have they changed?" In those cases, at least, the answer was, "No."

Real understanding of our "inner darknesses" must come from those levels of our awareness where they exist. We can't approach them only by way of the conscious mind, where they don't exist. A much better way of facing them is on a feeling, not an intellectual, level. This can be accomplished through action, and through actual experience — experience both of the negative aspects of one's faults, and of the positive aspects of their opposite virtues.

The intellect can be involved also. Eventually, of course, it must be. Few people, however, find it helpful to begin the struggle toward self-transformation at this end of the field. Self-analysis, when unaccompanied by direct, positive action, often becomes instead the first step toward self-paralysis.

The other reason that I've always had misgivings about the "face-the-darknesses" approach is that by concentrating too much on darkness one is likely to sink into despair. After all, it isn't as though this darkness were a mere veil, easily blown aside. By concentrating on it too minutely, moreover, we only magnify its size, even as amoebae loom large under a microscope.

The best way to rid ourselves of our inner darkness is to concentrate on that reality alone which is equipped to banish darkness: inner light. Armed with swords of light, we can take on the darknesses one at a time, and slay them. We can also, in the process, understand them a great deal more clearly than we ever could when examining them purely as shadows.

I had my doubts, therefore, when I visited this community of Jungian devotees. And my doubts proved more than justified.

The community members manifested no inner freedom from their "darknesses." Instead, they seemed overwhelmed by them. During the two days I was there I saw not one person smile. Grim-faced, tight-lipped, and staring at the ground about sums it all up. Later, I learned that there had been several suicides in the community — hushed up, but a burden on the group consciousness all the same.

The members challenged me on the point of my lighter outlook on things. I answered them with confidence.

Finally, their leader, after trying unsuccessfully to break down my defenses, exclaimed in exasperation, "My dear sir, you are *too* reasonable!"

If, by "reasonable," he meant that I chose to be guided by common sense, I must plead guilty.

This all applies to the arts in the sense that the artist can serve the cause of truth better if his view of reality is from a mountaintop rather than from the depths of a stagnant ditch.

A classmate of mine years ago, in college, informed me once that his mission in life was to write the Great American Novel.

"In what way do you want your novel to be great?" I inquired, intrigued that anyone would simply set out to write a great novel.

"Well, just great. I mean, you can't go beyond that in defining a thing, can you?"

"Well, for example: Do you want to feel the psychic pulse of America? Do you want to inspire people with a vision of America's greatness?"

"Inspire?" he inquired, frowning suspiciously. "What do you mean by that?"

"Well, for heaven's sake," I replied. "Inspiration can mean many things. For instance, it may mean helping people to become more sensitive to beauty."

"Beauty!" cried the great novelist, horror-stricken at my sentimentalism. "To the realist there is no such thing as beauty!"

Realism, then, to him, if it didn't mean a dull catalogue of dry facts, could only have meant an exposé of the seamier side of life. To him it more probably meant the latter, I thought, since that was the growing vogue. People, after all, who set out deliberately to write "great" novels are nothing if not voguish. I wondered whether his view of life had been acquired by lying in slum gutters on Saturday nights, taking notes. He didn't look as though fate had dragged him into any darkling abyss. It seemed to me obvious that, in the name of stark realism, he was merely embracing a fad.

For it is a common practice nowadays to dip pen or brush into the mud of squalor. The justification, supposedly, for sordid revelations is that honesty demands an unflinching gaze at the worst side of life. And so, as I said, it may. Between gazing unflinchingly, however, and fairly feasting the eyes one detects a subtle distinction.

There does in fact seem to be a marked tendency in this Twentieth Century for people, while denying beauty, to seek it again, perversely, in ugliness. One actually hears esthetes praise as "beautiful" paintings and poems that people of unconditioned tastes must surely view with repugnance.

Darwin may have been right when he traced our human ancestry back to the apes, but acceptance of this family tree has led to a great deal of moralistic doubletalk. People since Darwin's time have spoken as though human beings were merely monkeys in disguise. Not only is it considered priggish to ignore the beast in us; we are encouraged to denounce the angel as a hypocrite.

And yet, our aspirations represent us at least as truly as do our defects. A musician, struggling to master a difficult series of notes, hasn't expressed himself fully until the outward act finally matches his inward ideal. What, then, of the angel in us? Is it realistic to dismiss him as a dream, when no work of art was ever less so before it became a reality?

Novelists have tried to depict as "basic" human beings the very dregs of society, as though the remorseless honesty of such people had stripped them of the frills which an insincere and artificial age has imposed on the rest of us. Such people are endowed, supposedly, with the wisdom to see things *as they are.*

If, however, we study these heroes and heroines in real life — people who drink themselves into a stupor, or who give constant, free rein to violent tempers, or lead profligate lives, or indulge in other, similar, examples of "basic honesty" — we find weaklings, not realists: emotional adolescents whose lives are founded on delusions and lies.

To ignore the existence of the darker side of life would be unrealistic, obviously. But to *embrace* this darker side can only blind one to life's broader realities. Art that not only acknowledges, but fairly revels in, the sordid aspects of existence represents a step away from, not toward, whatever ultimate verities there be.

A work of art, as I've mentioned earlier in this book, ought to be something one can cherish, and not merely endure.

In life, it is natural to seek the company of people who inspire us. It is natural also to shun people who depress us. A work of art is cherished too, generally, not when it reveals the artist as lost, bewildered, and miserable, but when, through it, one feels he has something to say that can guide and inspire.

If, after reading a book, we conclude, "Well, this author certainly has his problems," we are unlikely to turn to him again except for that kind of company which misery seeks. Normally, what we want are solutions to our difficulties, not an increase of them. If the overall effect of a painting or a novel is depressing, we may safely say that its author hasn't yet achieved clarity in his vision of things.

For invariably accompanying the broad vision of Crystal Clarity is a disinclination for all in life that is petty or mean. Great art, inevitably, presents an exalted, not a debased, view of reality.

Chapter Fifteen

A Generous Spirit

What makes Shakespeare so much greater than Beaumont and Fletcher? Isn't it partly, at least, his generosity of spirit?

A study of the clearest and greatest minds of the ages reveals generosity, to varying degrees, in all of them. An expansive outlook always inspires tolerance. Small-mindedness and intolerance, on the other hand, are the primary symptoms of a nature that is petty and mean.

A great man — or a person of clear, honest vision — sees all things, including evil, from a standpoint of essential goodness. By this I don't mean he is naive. For there are two kinds of innocence: that kind which is born of mere lack of experience; and that which comes from having experienced everything, and understood it in its broadest context. That side of human nature which reaches out toward universal truths provides a much broader vision than that which comes from the narrow, "gut-level" focus of so many slum "realists."

An artist of real insight can take us through suffering and despair to an *expansion*, not a destruction, of inner peace. Through pain he awakens in us a broader sense of the mystery and beauty of life, an effect which Aristotle defined as *catharsis*. The starkest tragedy, penned with clear understanding, leaves one feeling cleansed, not pessimistic.

Pessimism is, in fact, incompatible with true clarity. For clarity implies wisdom. And wisdom is the mark of one who has learned to accept the world as it is, and himself as he is, accommodating himself to both — not in a spirit of complacency, but yet with a certain grace.

The broader the vision, the more positive it tends to be, not because it ignores the darknesses, but because it sees them as parts of a greater whole.

A generous and philosophical outlook unfolds automatically as one's vision expands beyond preoccupation with that favorite idol of immaturity, the strutting and self-proclaiming ego. The wise person's understanding of others derives not from callous judgment of them, but from a sense of their shared humanity with his own. His insight is born of deep kindness, compassion, and good humor. His wisdom arises naturally from a calm acceptance of life's vicissitudes.

Chapter Sixteen

A High Purpose

Modern science may, as some people claim, have weakened the foundations in logic for a purposive view of life, but this view remains nonetheless instinctive in all human greatness. Even the great men and women of science cannot avoid it; they betray their loyalty to it by their constant search for reasons and explanations, where lesser scientists are contented with the bare facts.

So it is that the greatest works of art always suggest a kind of spirituality. I don't mean they are necessarily religious. Spirituality is not a banner that people wave to proclaim which side they are on in the game of life. Nor is it an exclusive feature of the cloister. Rather, it is an all-pervasive ingredient of life itself — broader than any creed, too universal for monopoly by any church: an elusive something that may light for a time on the heart of an agnostic, or shun for a lifetime the prayers of an unloving believer.

In certain works of true art this spiritual outlook is openly professed. In others it is conveyed indirectly, as a subtle effect. In either case, however, from the pure, childlike music of Mozart, through the hidden power in the sculptures of Michelangelo, to the sublime mystical poems, in our age, of Paramhansa Yogananda, the strain is unfailingly present. It is the subtle breath of life, bestowing a magic charm on art forms which, in the hands of lesser men, remain forever vague and lifeless.

This is the last, the highest secret of Crystal Clarity. It is the highest secret of true genius.

A Selection of Other Books
by J. Donald Walters

Crises in Modern Thought — Solutions to the Problems of Meaninglessness. This book probes the discoveries of modern science for their pertinence to lasting human values.

Cities of Light — What Communities Can Accomplish, and the Need for Them in Our Times.

Rays of the Same Light — Parallel Passages, with Commentary, From the Bible and the Bhagavad Gita.

The Art of Supportive Leadership — a practical handbook for people in positions of responsibility.

Education for Life — a book on childhood education.

The Search — A Young Person's Quest for Understanding. This autobiography is a deeply moving revelation of a poignant search for truth.

The Story of Crystal Hermitage — the building of a home, and a life.

How To Be a Channel — how to truly transmit inspiration received from sources other than the ego.

Secrets of Happiness — daily thoughts for the month.

Affirmations and Prayers — a collection of 52 spiritual qualities, a discussion of each, with an affirmation and prayer for its realization.

The Land of Golden Sunshine — a poetic parable.

On Wings of Joy — songs and poems of Divine Joy.

Ring, Bluebell, Ring! — songs and poems for children.

J. Donald Walters resides at Ananda World Brotherhood Village, the spiritual community he founded in 1968. Ananda is one of the most successful intentional communities in the world. For further information about the community, its guest programs, or a product brochure, please write the publisher, or call 916-292-3065.

Crystal Clarity —
a new concept in living

Crystal Clarity means to see oneself, and all things, as aspects of a greater reality; to seek to enter into conscious attunement with that reality; and to see all things as channels for the expression of that reality.

It means to see truth in simplicity; to seek always to be guided by the simple truth, not by opinion; and by what *is*, not by one's own desires or prejudices.

It means striving to see things in relation to their broadest potential.

In one's association with other people, it means seeking always to include their realities in one's own.